Field Guide to the Northeast Alpine Summits

Field Guide to the Northeast Alpine Summits

Maine, New Hampshire, Vermont, and New York

Allison W. Bell & Nancy G. Slack

Printed in the United States of America
ISBN 978-1-62534-989-7

Book and cover design by Allison W. Bell.
All photographs by Allison W. Bell, except those listed on page 204.
Printed by Bookmobile.

Distributed for Allison W. Bell by Mill River Books.

Cover: Lapland rosebay and diapensia blooming on Chandler Ridge, Mount Washington. Page 2: Mountain avens flowering along the Alpine Garden Trail, Mount Washington.

CONTENTS

PREFACE

THE MOUNTAINS of the northeastern United States have some of the most interesting and beautiful alpine vegetation in America, as well as birds, insects, and other animals that make this special place their home.

This world exists in its greatest diversity and exuberance on Mount Washington and the Presidential Range and on Mounts Lafayette and Lincoln on Franconia Ridge in New Hampshire. Elsewhere in the region, the alpine areas are smaller and more scattered. The most important are Katahdin and other high summits in northern Maine, Mount Mansfield and Camel's Hump in Vermont, and Mount Marcy and several high peaks in New York's Adirondacks. Many species found on these alpine summits can be found on lower ones as well, even on those that barely reach 4,000 feet. To hike through all the lower mountain forest zones and finally arrive at the summit is the most satisfying way to view the alpine zone, but this is not the only option. Roads go nearly to the top of Mount Mansfield and Whiteface Mountain. You can also reach Mount Washington's summit by driving or by taking the Cog Railway. For an overnight experience,

▲ The Crawford Path up Mount Washington takes you through some of the most glorious alpine habitat in the northeastern United States.

you can stay in or near the alpine zone by visiting the Appalachian Mountain Club (AMC) huts, which provide food and lodging.

The native alpine plants and animals survive in a very difficult environment. Mount Washington has some of the most extreme weather in the country, even in summer. On any of the Northeast's alpine summits, we humans must come equipped for changeable, sometimes dangerous conditions, but species native to the alpine have evolved to withstand them on their own. Still, this habitat is fragile. Unwary hikers can trample rare and endangered plants, and climate change is upsetting delicate balances throughout the ecosystem. In this guide you will get to know the plants and animals that inhabit this zone and understand something of their lives in their alpine surroundings.

This book is the culmination of 35 years of partnership between Nancy Slack and myself, producing field guides for the alpine areas of New England and New York. Our first publication, *85 Acres* (1992), covered the high peak summits in the Adirondacks, where both of us began our life-long fascination with the world above treeline. That book was followed by *Field Guide to the New England Alpine Summits* (1995), updated in 2006, with a new edition in 2016. In 2007, we published *Adirondack Alpine Summits,* an expanded version of our first work. Nancy and I had long discussed a combined field guide, covering all of the Northeast alpine areas. These high mountains across the region share many of the same species and the same ecology. They also share visitors, and face the

Nancy Slack surveys alpine snowbed communities on Mount Washington, 2014. ▼

▲ Nancy Slack and Allison Bell lead naturalists and summit steward trainees on a trip to the alpine zone on New York's Mount Haystack, 1993.

same challenges, changes and threats.

In this field guide, you will find photos and descriptions of more than 200 mountain species—flowering plants, mosses, lichens, amphibians, mammals, butterflies, and other animals. The scientific names of flowering plants have been updated to match those in the Native Plant Trust's *Flora Novae Angliae* by Arthur Haines (second edition, 2026). There are special expanded entries for some of the most unusual and interesting plants and animals you will find on these mountaintops. The Flowering Chart (p. 194) will help you identify alpine flowers by color and bloom date. The chapters on conservation and phenology have been updated to include new research and reports from ongoing conservation projects.

This book project has benefited from the expertise and encouragement from longtime colleague and alpine researcher Robert Capers. Since Nancy's death in 2024, he has generously assisted with scientific input, editing, and contributions to the section on climate change.

We are especially concerned with the preservation of alpine plants and animals in the face of environmental threats. Hopefully, in learning to identify the flora and fauna of the Northeast's alpine zones, you'll share our interest and get involved. Citizen conservation efforts such as AMC's Northeast Alpine Flower Watch program give you a chance to help monitor the delicate balance of life on the highest peaks of Vermont, New Hampshire, Maine, and the Adirondack mountains. The more information we have about the health of these rare communities, the better chance we have of saving them for generations to come.

—*Allison Bell*

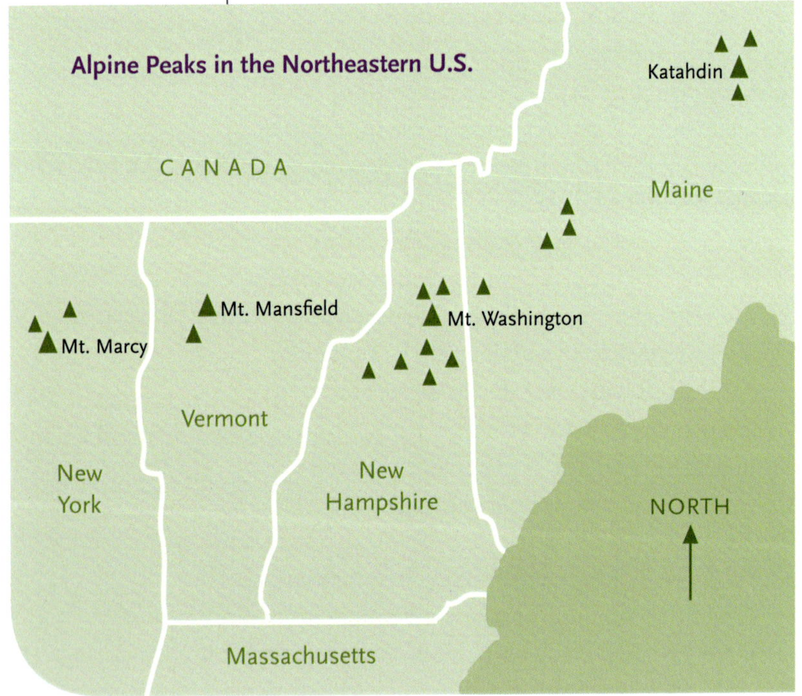

INTRODUCTION

THIS BOOK WILL TAKE YOU, in images and text, up the highest mountain ranges in New Hampshire, Maine, Vermont and New York. We will climb to 6,288 feet on Mount Washington and to over 5,000 feet on its neighboring peaks in the Presidential Range. We'll travel nearly as high on Franconia Ridge, to 5,344 feet on Mount Marcy and 5,267 feet on Katahdin in Maine. Vermont's Mount Mansfield is only 4,393 feet above sea level, but it has a very extensive alpine ridge. We will begin at the trailheads and climb through several forest zones—to treeline and above. Although each of these zones has its own diverse and fascinating ecology, our main focus is on life on the summits.

Spruce-fir forest and krummholz zones lead up to the alpine summit of 5,774-foot Mount Adams. ▼

In order to understand something of the varied mountain landscape, you need to know how it came to be—its geological evolution. In order to survive up there, you need some knowledge of the weather, especially the famous conditions on Mount Washington. But first, a bit of history.

EARLY EXPLORATIONS

BEFORE EUROPEAN CONTACT, Native people lived among the Northeast's mountains for millennia, but there is no material evidence of their climbing to the summits or making use of resources from high elevations. The first recorded ascent into the region's alpine zones was in 1642. English settler Darby Field and two Native companions climbed "the White Hill" (later named Mount Washington) after a long trip up the Saco River from the coast. Field claimed to have found precious minerals on the mountain, which turned out to be mica and quartz, not diamonds. In 1772, Ira Allen, younger brother of Revolutionary War hero Ethan Allen, climbed Mount Mansfield and ran a survey line across the crest of the ridge. It was not until 1804 that surveyor Charles Turner recorded the first ascent of Katahdin. To climb these wilderness peaks before there were trails, maps, or approach roads was an awesome feat.

◄ Alpine azalea and diapensia were among the arctic plants eagerly sought by early explorers on Northeast summits.

Quartz and mica are common components of the rocks in the Presidential Range. ▼

Early scientific exploration of the Northeast's alpine peaks centered on Mount Washington. In July 1784, Manasseh Cutler, Massachusetts minister and noted botanist, led an expedition aimed at climbing and exploring the "great mountain." The party included future clergyman and historian Jeremy Belknap along with other men of varied scientific interests. They were the first to make physical measurements on the summit, which they estimated to be 10,000 feet above sea level—nearly 4,000 feet taller than it really is. It was 44°F on the cloud-shrouded "Sugar-loaf" and their heavy instruments were not working well. The group got lost on their way down, probably descending via treacherous Huntington Ravine, and spent the night unprepared, huddled around a fire.

In 1804, Cutler returned to now-named Mount Washington with mathematician and astronomer Nathaniel Bowditch and botanist William Peck. Cutler and Peck found alpine plants new to science, including an alpine goldenrod (now named Cutler's goldenrod) which also grows on Katahdin, Mount Mansfield, and the Adirondacks' highest peaks, and mountain avens, a showy June flower found only in the White Mountains and Nova Scotia.

The Alpine Garden, a level area on the shoulder of Mount Washington, has attracted botanists for over 200 years.▼

In 1811, Lieutenant Alden Partridge climbed Mount Washington by a route that would later become the Crawford Path. An indefatigable hiker, he eventually measured the heights of many New Hampshire mountains and other New England peaks. At almost the same time, mineralogist Colonel George Gibbs laid out the first path from the east, probably through Tuckerman Ravine. Most early climbers, including an ever-growing number of botanists, used this route. In 1819, local guides Abel and Ethan Allen Crawford cut an eight-mile trail over the Southern Presidentials to Lakes of the Clouds and the summit of Mount Washington. Today the Crawford Path is the oldest continuously used hiking trail in the Northeast. A journey along its route will reveal a great many alpine plants and other features that are shown in this book.

▲ Established trails made access easier to the mountaintops, especially through the krummholz zone—impenetrable thickets of dwarf trees.

Two excellent botanists arrived in 1816 to explore the mountain—Jacob Bigelow and Francis Boott. Bigelow was a newly appointed Harvard professor; Boott was a Harvard graduate and later became a famous London physician. Bigelow wrote a fascinating account of the White Mountains for the *New England Journal of Medicine and Surgery*, discussing Mount Washington geology and describing three vegetative zones on the mountain:

> *The predominance of rocks [in the alpine zone] leaves but a scanty surface covered with soil capable of giving root to vegetation; yet to the*

WHAT'S IN A NAME?

Mount Washington's famous flora attracted a great many scientists during the 1800s and their names remain. Did you know these features were named for men who studied alpine plants here?

botanist this is by far the most interesting part of the mountain. Many of the plants of this region are rare. . . . Among them are natives of Siberia, of Lapland, of Greenland and Labrador.

Bigelow listed plants found "on the uppermost portion" of Mount Washington, including those found by Boott, whose "botanical zeal induced him to undertake a second visit to the summit in August." The list notes either July 2 or August 25 for the blooming of each plant, the first time that Northeast alpine flowering dates were recorded in print. The intrepid botanists William Oakes, a Massachusetts lawyer, and James Robbins, a Massachusetts physician, explored the Presidential Range in the 1820s. The botanically rich gulf beneath Mount Monroe bears Oakes's name, as does an alpine eyebright he discovered there, *Euphrasia oakesii*. Oakes named the globally rare Robbins' or dwarf cinquefoil, which grows nearby, for his "excellent friend."

▲ Early botanists collected and pressed samples for study, even of this rare Robbins' cinquefoil from 1924. Today it is illegal to collect any alpine plants without a special research permit.

More visitors came to Mount Washington in the 1820s, and most stuck to the established paths. But, as local innkeeper Lucy Crawford wrote, "one class of visitors began to wander off trail, and indeed into every nook and cranny of the range." These were the botanists, and probably more of them explored the White Mountains in the twenty years following 1825 than at any time since.

Perhaps best remembered is Edward Tuckerman —of Ravine fame—who began his Mount Washington explorations in 1837. A graduate of Union College in Schenectady, New York, he also earned graduate degrees at Harvard and was a professor at Amherst College. Well known for his study of the alpine flower-

▲ Mount Mansfield's summit can be climbed by several trails, or by taking the toll road and hiking along the summit ridge to the top.

ing plants, he became one of the first experts on North American lichens.

Tuckerman returned many times to the Presidential Range, and, along with University of Vermont graduate William Macrae, explored the alpine areas of Vermont in 1839. Other early botanists with experience on Mount Washington surveyed here, too. Zadock Thompson's 1853 edition of *History of Vermont* (Burlington, VT: By the author) includes a plant list compiled by William Oakes for the state. It explains that "the summits of Mansfield and Camel's Hump have been pretty thoroughly examined by Dr. Robbins, Mr. Tuckerman, and Mr. Macrae." Although they found fewer alpine plants than on the much higher Presidential Range, Oakes lists many alpine species, including black crowberry, bearberry willow, and fir clubmoss.

Because of Katahdin's remote location, scientific exploration on Maine's highest peak was slower to get underway. In August 1804, before the state was separated from Massachusetts, surveyors were sent into the largely unmapped Maine woods. Charles Turner and ten men approached "Catardin" in canoes and climbed the ridge that the Hunt Trail now follows. In a letter about his journey, Turner noted the coarse-grain crumbling rock and the dwarf trees that "came to nothing at about a half mile from the summit" and described the view from the top as "enchanting." At sundown, the team began their descent, leaving behind a lead sheet incised with their initials and a corked bottle of rum.

Only a handful of determined parties had climbed the still wild and trailless woods of Katahdin by 1837. That year, geologist Charles Thomas Jackson ascended the peak by the Abol Slide in wild, wet weather. In 1845, Harvard graduate Edward Everett Hale and hiking companion William Francis Channing—both with impressive White Mountain climbing experience—set off to attempt Katahdin from the north.

Katahdin's slopes rise abruptly from the surrounding landscape, affording magnificent views, when the weather allows. ▼

Asa Gray, the famous Harvard botanist, expressed interest in comparing the flora of Mount Washington and Katahdin, and Hale agreed to collect samples for him from the mountain's alpine areas. After many days spent just approaching the mountain and a strenuous climb through "terribly impassable" krummholz, the two young men and their guide enjoyed a summit prospect "as wild and grand as God made it." They camped above treeline and set out the following morning to explore the mountain. As the "clouds were thicker and thicker, and the rain worse and worse," the party retreated downhill. Despite the weather, Hale returned to Massachusetts with more than 400 dried and pressed alpine plant specimens for scientific study.

As early explorers testified, exposed rock and changeable weather make Katahdin a challenging climb. ▼

Henry David Thoreau visited Katahdin in 1846 and left us a wonderful journal, including descriptions of the plants he saw. He got as far as the Tableland plateau on Baxter Peak's western face, "deep within the hostile ranks of clouds," but was forced to descend without reaching the summit.

The next year, Aaron Young commenced the first botanical survey of Maine with an expedition to Katahdin. The party reached the top, where "Dr. Young, though much fatigued, enjoyed this rare opportunity for gathering Alpine plants." Another member of the group observed mountain sandwort, which he mused "only lived here because it was nearer heaven, to gaze freely at the stars, and catch the first glance at the sun's golden eye."

▲ Mounts Colden and Marcy viewed from Algonquin Peak. Scientific exploration of the Adirondack alpine areas began in the 1830s.

European explorers Samuel de Champlain and Henry Hudson both glimpsed the Adirondack high peaks in 1608, but the first Adirondack peak was not officially climbed for more than 200 years.

In 1836, New York Governor William L. Marcy authorized a survey of the Adirondack wilderness, with geologists Ebenezer Emmons and James Hall in charge. That September, Emmons and Hall climbed Whiteface and measured its height at over 4,800 feet. They returned the next summer, along with botanist John Torrey, to pursue the geological survey and to climb Mount Marcy. The party camped at 3,700 feet, and early on August 5, 1837, this group scrambled through the dwarf trees of the krummholz zone and at last reached Marcy's summit, "covered only with mosses and small alpine plants."

New York State Surveyor Verplanck Colvin conducted the most important exploration of the High Peaks. As Superintendent of the Adirondack Topographical Survey for 28 years, he and and his assistant, Joseph Blake, summited and measured a

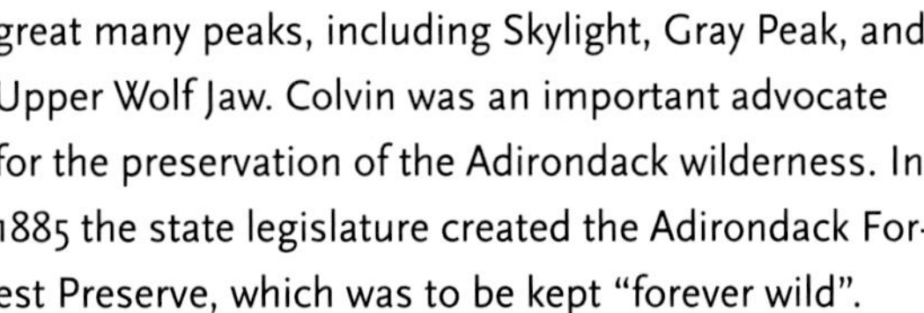

great many peaks, including Skylight, Gray Peak, and Upper Wolf Jaw. Colvin was an important advocate for the preservation of the Adirondack wilderness. In 1885 the state legislature created the Adirondack Forest Preserve, which was to be kept "forever wild".

By the 1850s, visitors were able to ride on horseback up Mount Washington, as they did on Mount Lafayette and other Northeast peaks. Summit houses for overnight guests were built during this period on Mount Washington, Mount Mansfield, and Moosilauke. The midcentury rise in mountain tourism coincided with popular interest in nature study and botanizing. When the Mount Washington Carriage Road was completed in 1861 and the cog railroad carried its first passengers up in 1869, tourists arrived by the carload—botanizers among them. Entomologist Annie T. Slosson described these enthusiasts as flying "from side to side of the train car, looking eagerly out and uttering strange exclamations, such as 'Geum!', 'Ledum!' . . . springing from the train at its brief stops to collect plants to the intense amazement and amusement of the unscientific passengers."

Alice Rich Northrop, with a metal plant-collecting vasculum. She and husband John Northrop spent a week botanizing on Mount Washington in early July 1889 and found more than 60 different plants in flower above 4,600 feet. ▼

During the last decades of the century, recreational climbers and botanizers were an increasing part of the Northeast alpine scene—and many were women. Notable among these were Lucia Pychowska and her daughter Marian. In 1864, with Adirondack guide "Old Mountain" Phelps, Lucia climbed Mount Marcy via Ausable Lakes. She wrote enthusiastically about her hike to the summit where "the clouds all rolled away . . . and left us the most glorious view our eyes had ever rested upon." Through the 1880s, with family and friends who included early members of the Appalachian Mountain Club, Lucia and Maria explored little-known corners of the White Mountains. They helped build trails, studied mountain flora, and wrote of their experiences in *Appalachia* journal. Lucia offered advice to her sister mountaineers: Pin up your long skirt (worn over wool trousers) to ascend steep trails or "transit through hobble bush." Release it afterward for modesty. She had scrambled over the entire Presidential Range and down Tuckerman Ravine in such an outfit. Lucia boasted that at the end of these climbs she appeared "sufficiently presentable to enter a hotel without attracting uncomfortable attention."

Mountain avens, *Geum peckii*

Marian Pychowska wrote of the alpine zone: "a paradise of deep moss and fairy-like plants." On one June climb up King Ravine, she delighted to find "legions of alpine heather-bells," "banks of diapensia," and "a few of the geums' golden butter-plates" in bloom.

Today, visitors to the alpine zone can still travel the old roads or the Mount Washington Cog Railway in pursuit of natural wonders. The legacy of early explorers and scientists is honored, in part, in the geography, plant, and animal names of the region—from the Cutler River and Bigelow Lawn to Robbins' cinquefoil and Boott's rattlesnake-root. There are no longer bridle paths or summit hotels, but you can hike the many trails above treeline, perhaps stay in an AMC hut, and be surrounded by alpine flowers.

▲ One of the dried specimens gathered by botanizers Marian and Lucia Pychowska from the Presidential Range in 1886. The collection was on display for members' reference at the Appalachian Mountain Club headquarters in Boston.

THE GEOLOGICAL EVENTS lleading to the formation of the Northeast's mountains started more than one billion years ago. The process involved plate tectonics—the shifting layers of the earth's outer crust which have collided over the eons to produce volcanoes, earthquakes, new mountain ranges, oceans, and continents. Much more recent events, such as the period when even the tops of Mounts Washington, Mansfield, Marcy and Katahdin were covered by glacial ice, have also made dramatic changes in the mountain landscape.

▲ Mount Monroe is a *roche moutonnée*—smooth on one side where glaciers wore it down, and jagged on the other.

◀ One of two Lakes of the Clouds, glacial tarns high on Mount Washington.

Adirondack High Peaks are made of anorthosite, a billion-year-old rock. ▼

On the highest Adirondack peaks, the rock you walk on is more than a billion years old, an ancient dome of uplifted metamorphic rock. It was once covered with layers of sedimentary rock miles thick that gradually eroded. The High Peaks are still getting higher, at a rate of about 2–3 millimeters per year.

In New England, the first of two major mountain-building events, called the Taconic orogeny, took place 460 million years ago. At that time a volcanic island chain, represented today by the Ammonoosuc formation (found at the base of Mount Madison), rose from an ocean called Iapetus, a precursor of the Atlantic. The island chain collided with what was then the margin of North America (now the Adirondacks), folding undersea sediments of Iapetus to form the Green Mountains of Vermont.

The second orogeny, called the Acadian, took place approximately 400 million years ago. Europe, Africa, and the Americas collided, closing Iapetus and forming the supercontinent Pangaea (a name meaning "all lands"). The continental shift buried marine sediments consisting of sands and mud under Iapetus deeply in the earth. There, intense heat and pressure metamorphosed them into quartzite and schist, respectively. The metamorphosed rock was folded, then thrust up into tall ranges to become the Appalachian Mountains, including the Presidential Range with its Littleton and Rangeley formations. When young, the Appalachians may have been as high as the present-day Himalayas.

Cairns built of schist and topped with white quartz rocks help hikers find their way on the many foggy days in the Presidential Range. ▼

Although New Hampshire is called "The Granite State" (because much of its rock is just that), the majority of the Presidential Range is not. Where the underground heat and pressure was particularly intense, mica and quartz separated into discrete black-and-white bands to form gneiss (pronounced "nice"). Some Littleton schists under intense heat "sweated out" their quartz, resulting in the milky, snowy white quartz most noticeable in the "moon rock" near Star Lake, between Mounts Adams and Madison. Schist, gneiss, and quartz are on display throughout the Presidential Range.

During the Jurassic Period, about 200 million years ago, a high point of dinosaur life on earth, Pangaea was splitting apart, creating the current Atlantic Ocean. Volcanoes formed and erupted, spewing igneous rock that makes up, for example, the Moat and Ossipee ranges southeast of the Presidentials. Mount Lafayette above Franconia Notch exemplifies an intrusive dike, another kind of igneous formation, which is the result of molten rock, or magma, filling a rock fracture and then cooling. Igneous rock that remained below the surface cooled into the coarse-grained granite for which New Hampshire is famous. Such a mass of granite, formed deep within the earth and then exposed by erosion and uplift, is called a pluton. Today plutons of granite can be seen in the Conway region and in the Crawford Notch and Zealand areas. The Katahdin Range in Baxter State Park in northern Maine is another such pluton. Katahdin itself is

The Katahdin Range is a pluton, a mass of granite formed deep in the earth and later exposed. ▼

▲ The Great Gulf is a steep-walled glacial cirque on Mount Washington.

overlain by a resistant rock cap of granophyre, much harder than even the coarse granite below.

The tectonic uplifts were accompanied and followed by erosion that have sculpted the Northeast's mountains into the forms we see today. Mountain streams running down the steep slopes carved deep V-shaped valleys such as the Ammonoosuc Ravine. As the climate cooled, valley glaciers formed from snow buildup at the higher elevations that became ice and flowed downhill. On Mount Washington, valley glaciers carved into the mountain to form glacial cirques—Tuckerman and Huntington Ravines—with towering headwalls. Most cirques in the Adirondacks and New England are found on the east and north sides of mountains because the prevailing winds cause great accumulations of winter snow in those areas. On Katahdin's east side are large glacial cirques, with steep 2,300-foot headwalls. Katahdin's Cathedral Ridge and Knife Edge are narrow ridges, or arêtes, separating two cirque basins.

The Pleistocene glaciers began forming approximately two million years ago. During the Wisconsin period of the Pleistocene epoch, 50,000 years ago, continental ice sheets covered everything—the ice sheet over the top of Mount Washington and all the other peaks was more than a mile thick. Evidence of their passing can be seen in surface scratches called glacial striae and scour marks left on exposed bedrock. These striae indicate the glaciers' thickness and the direction they flowed—northwest to southeast in the Presidentials. Continental glaciers also scooped out long U-shaped valleys such as the Crawford Notch and Zealand Notch, while the epoch's valley glaciers carved similarly shaped valleys such as the Great Gulf on Mount Washington's north side.

The bedrock on Adirondack high peak summits has been worn smooth by glacial action. ▼

When the last glacier melted about 11,000 years ago it left behind the stones, dirt, and debris it was carrying. In the White Mountains this glacial till is a foot or two thick. It is found throughout the region—even on the summit of Mount Washington. Much of the mountain soil, including coarse sand, clay, and angular stones, is made up of this glacial till.

Other evidence of glacial advance and retreat can be seen in roches moutonnées, asymmetrical landforms also called sheepbacks or whalebacks. In the Presidentials, Mount Monroe is a giant roche moutonnée—smooth on the northwest slope, where glaciers wore it down, and jagged on the southeast, where the glaciers' advance tore off chunks of rock. Lakes of the Clouds on Mount Washington and Lake Tear of the Clouds on Mount Marcy are examples of tarns—basins scooped out by glacial ice.

Huge boulders called glacial erratics were carried by the ice sheets, and left behind as the glaciers melted. Boulders could be transported great distances and thus differ from the local bedrock. Glacial erratics are found throughout the Northeast—some high above treeline. The renowned Glen Boulder on Mount Washington is a glacial erratic; it was moved from the Randolph area, northwest of the mountain, to its present location.

Alternate freezing and thawing loosened rock at the joints and broke away the top layer, resulting in striking, angular formations such as the former Old Man of the Mountain. Felsenmeers—slopes of jagged angular boulders—take shape as freeze-thaw

Felsenmeer, or "sea of rocks," stripped off the underlying bedrock by freeze-thaw weathering. ▼

▲ Soil stripes on Bigelow Lawn on Mount Washington. These are not tracks made by people but a natural alpine phenomenon caused by frost action at high elevations.

weathering breaks up the top rock into jumbled chunks. Trails across felsenmeer can be difficult to negotiate with a pack, especially in a strong wind.

Freezing and thawing of rocks and the movement of soil, a process called solifluction, formed a variety of patterned ground features above treeline. Stone circles or polygons, soil stripes, and terraces are the result of differential movement of coarse and fine material. Most of these are rock patterns formed in the severe postglacial climate, but similar phenomena still occur today in areas of considerable frost action. Soil stripes are a natural phenomenon; you can see them on Bigelow Lawn on Mount Washington. Solifluction creates unique microhabitats especially suited to alpine plants such as Robbins' cinquefoil and mountain sandwort.

By 11,000 years ago, the glaciers had largely melted away, and southern New York and New England were free of ice. There were no trees; the landscape looked like the Arctic tundra. New soils were formed and retained with the help of pioneering lichens and mosses, then colonized by arctic plants. As the climate warmed, conifers and eventually deciduous trees migrated north. Spruces and firs dominated the higher slopes, crowding out the once-widespread arctic tundra plants, now left on very special "islands" on our coldest summits. Alpine vegetation now grows only above 4,500 feet and at somewhat lower elevations where there are exposed windswept sites. Above treeline, there have been alpine plant communities for 10,000 years. The spruce and fir forests below have almost all been lumbered; even what we call "old growth" forest is less than 200 years old. Thus, the alpine summits are living museums—truly old communities—to be explored, enjoyed, and protected.

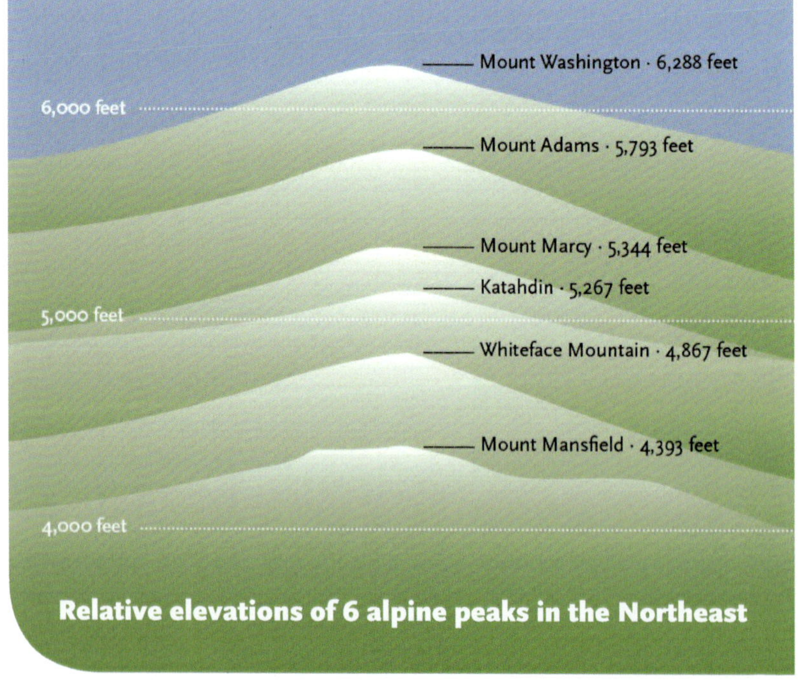

Relative elevations of 6 alpine peaks in the Northeast

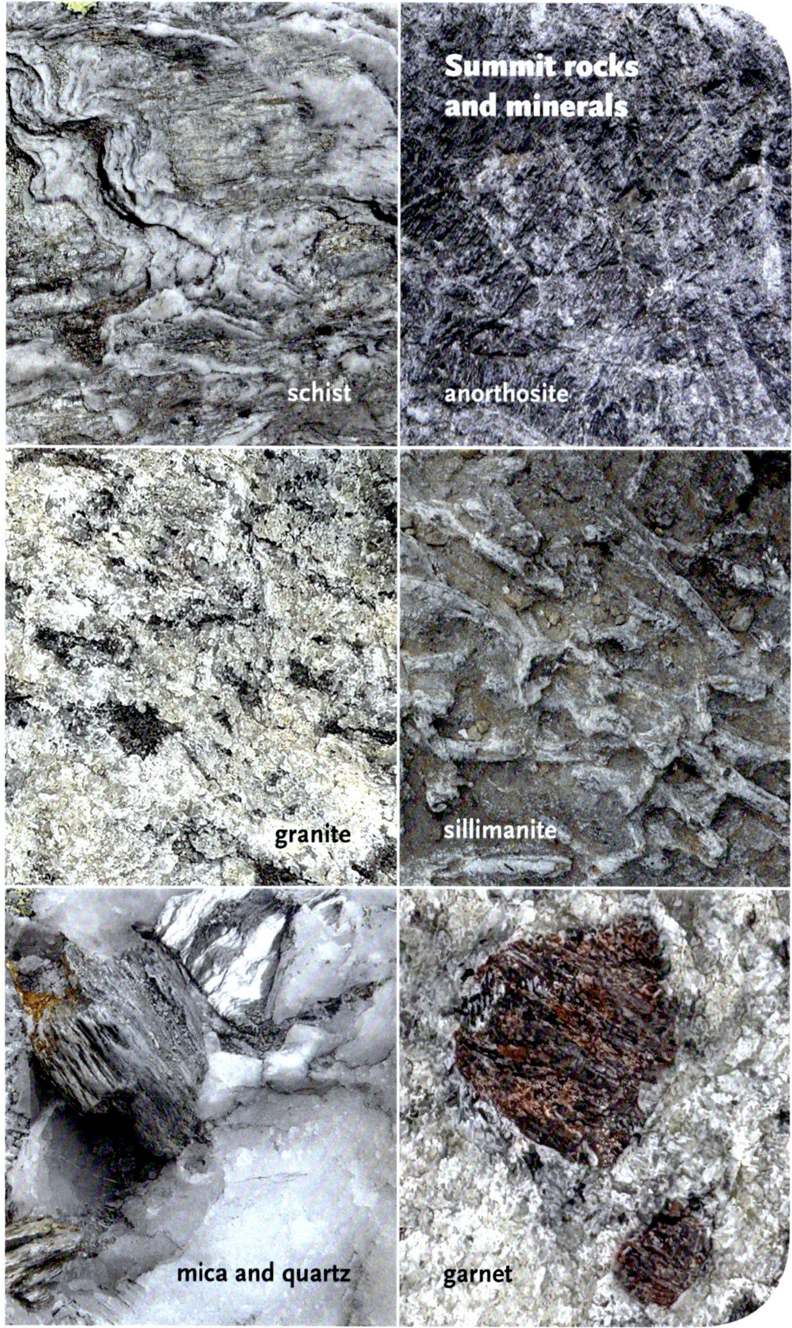
Summit rocks
and minerals
schist
anorthosite
granite
sillimanite
mica and quartz
garnet

◀ A summer day on Mount Washington—snow and ice can occur any day of the year.

SEVENTEENTH-CENTURY visitors called the Northern Presidentials "daunting terrible" and the surrounding forest "a vast and howling wilderness." Today the mountain weather remains just as impressive and severe. Since 1855, when a young climber named Lizzie Bourne fell victim to a September storm, close to 150 people have perished on Mount Washington alone, many from weather-related causes. What is it about this mountain's weather and climate that can make it so dangerous?

First, there are the hurricane-force winds. Wind speeds exceed 100 mph every month of the year. The strongest surface wind ever recorded in the Northern Hemisphere, 231 mph, was clocked by the Mount Washington Observatory in 1934. (A wind speed of 253 mph was recorded in a tropical cyclone in Australia in 1996, breaking the record for the highest wind speed, but Mount Washington can still claim the "world's worst weather.") Hurricane winds of more than 75 mph occur on half of all winter days and two to four days each summer month. Both authors have experienced such wind speeds—and higher—

Thick fog and strong winds make hiking a challenge above treeline. ▼

on Mount Washington in summer.

And then there is the temperature. The average July temperature is 49°F; the January mean is 5°F. Very often the temperature on top of Mount Washington is 30 or more degrees colder than the temperature at its base. This is because air masses rise when they hit the mountain barrier. With decreased atmospheric pressure at higher elevations, the air expands and cools. An average 3°F temperature drop occurs with every 1,000-foot increase in elevation. In any summer month, you can start up Mount Washington comfortable in shorts and a T-shirt and find yourself in subfreezing conditions above treeline. A visit to the alpine flowers in June requires being prepared for challenging weather. In winter, with the average windchill factored in, exposed skin can freeze in one minute. Climbers take note!

Strong winds toss cotton sedges at Star Lake near Mount Madison. Winds can toss hikers here, too—hurricane-force blasts are not uncommon above treeline.▼

If you are going to be above treeline, even in July and August, you will need protection from wind, driving rain, sleet and even snow. A waterproof jacket, pants, and warm layers are essential. Although the summit is in clouds 75 percent of the time, you can still get sunburned, so bring sunscreen and sunglasses. Other necessities, if only for a day trip, are good hiking boots, food, water, and a small first-aid kit. Bring your phone for photos, but do not count on it for emergency communication, light or trail navigation. Bring a working flashlight and a paper map—many search and rescue incidents involve lost hikers stranded at nightfall with failing phones. Common sense, caution, and preparation are needed in all of the Northeast's alpine areas, particularly during bad weather on Mount Washington and on Katahdin's Knife Edge. A summer morning in sunshine can swiftly degrade into and afternoon of fog, icy rain, and nasty wind. The alpine plants and animals cope with these changes much better than we humans do.

▲ A weather warning sign cautions hikers approaching the alpine zone on Mount Washington—"The weather ahead is the worst in North America."

Witnessing extreme weather was the intended goal of geologists Charles Hitchcock and Joshua Huntington, who collaborated on the first extended winter occupation of Mount Washington's summit for scientific work. Huntington (for whom Huntington Ravine is named) and Hitchcock made observations from atop Moosilauke in the winter of 1869–70. They arranged with the U.S. Army Signal Service and the Cog Railway to begin scientific studies on Mount

Washington in the fall of 1870. A telegraph wire was strung to the summit, and equipment was sent up by the Cog Railway and carriage road. Huntington arrived first at the summit station and made weather observations, telegraphing them to Professor Hitchcock at Dartmouth College. On November 3, 1870, four men, including two photographers, were climbing Mount Washington to join Huntington when the weather suddenly changed:

> *[W]hen the storm struck. . . . There were suddenly wrapped around us dense clouds of frozen vapor, driven so furiously into our faces by the raging winds as to threaten suffocation. The cheering repose of a moment before had now given place to what might well be felt as the power and hoarse rage of a thousand furies; the shroud of darkness . . . was in a moment thrown over us. . . . The cloud of frozen vapor that lashed us so furiously as it hugged us in its chilling embrace, was so dense that no object could be seen at a distance of ten paces.*[1]

Weather scientists endured the bitter winter conditions on Mount Washington in 1870–71, as shown in *Harper's Weekly*. ▼

Huntington, Hitchcock, and their crew were the first to put together major records of the mountain's weather conditions and to try to improve weather forecasting, then in its scientific infancy. The summit was occupied by the Signal Service from 1871 to 1892, and hardy Dartmouth students apparently stayed the winter as well, surviving a temperature of –59°F and a wind speed of 186 mph, the highest recorded at that time. The station was finally abandoned,

▲ Undercast and dramatic clouds at the top of Huntington Ravine

and in 1908 this early weather bureau burnt down.

After this the Mount Washington Observatory was established in 1932 and is still operating. All subsequent meteorology and climatology on Mount Washington has been dependent on the pioneering work of Hitchcock, Huntington, and their associates.

A great deal of attention has been devoted recently to climate change and its effects on the Northeast's alpine flora and fauna. One study showed that treeline elevations in the Presidential Range and on Mount Katahdin have risen an average of three meters per decade for the past 40 years. As on alpine summits elsewhere in the world, climate change seems to be driving increases in shrubs and declines in mosses and some herbaceous plants. Long-term monitoring now is being done on a regular basis in the White Mountains and in two mountain ranges in Québec—the Chic-Chocs and the Uapishka—

▲ Diapensia with flowers frozen by a fierce June ice storm

recording changes and trying to understand the relationships between warming and other conditions. An additional monitoring site is also planned in the Adirondacks.

On Mount Washington, research done by AMC suggests that high winds, very frequent cloud cover, and rime ice may prevent the current warming trends at lower elevations from encroaching into the higher altitudes in the Presidential Range of New Hampshire. Here, flowering has begun earlier, but the average flowering date has only moved from June 13 to June 12. Continuing climate change may, however, endanger flora in the lower, narrower alpine zones on Mount Mansfield and Katahdin, as well as the Adirondacks, where the winds are not so strong and the cloud cover less persistent.

Stationary lenticular clouds formed by warm air passing over Mount Washington's summit ▼

The Northern Hardwood Forest Zone

To get to the alpine zones of New England and New York, you will travel through several other mountain environments: northern hardwood forest, spruce-fir forest, and balsam fir forest. You can begin your climb at many points for the ascent of the Presidentials, Franconia Ridge, Mounts Marcy or Mansfield, or Katahdin. This account concentrates on the Mount Washington routes, but trailheads are similar elsewhere. You might begin your climb of Mount Washington, for example, at around 1,300 feet on the Appalachian Trail (Webster Cliff Trail) at NH 302 in Crawford Notch. At this elevation, you find yourself in the northern hardwood forest. This is a largely deciduous forest, blazing with color in late September and early October, and dominated by sugar maple, American beech with smooth gray bark, and yellow birch with peeling bark gleaming like brass candlesticks in the autumn sun. Other trees live here, too, including red maple, black cherry, red oak, aspen, paper birch, white pine, and hemlock, as well as a great variety of shrubs, ferns, and wildflowers.

Almost all trails to alpine summits in Northeast begin in the northern hardwood forest, home to a great diversity of plants, birds, and other animals. ▼

▲ Painted trilliums (top) and the white form *(albidiflorum)* of the pink lady-slipper (above)

Wild sarsaparilla is common in the northern hardwood forest, as is red trillium. Striking painted trillium, white with magenta streaks, and the double-decker Indian cucumber-root are characteristic spring flowers. So are many species of violets, flowering in white, blue, and even yellow. Watch for pink (sometimes white) lady-slipper orchids with pleated oval leaves blooming in June. Look and photograph, but do not pick. Hobblebush is a conspicuous shrub, with large, almost heart-shaped leaves and bright red berries in late summer. Like a number of plants and animals of the northern hardwood forest zone, it may also be found higher up into the transition forest zone. Some species are able to survive into the spruce-fir forest zone, and a versatile few, such as Canada mayflower, bluebead lily, and starflower, appear all the way up into sheltered habitats in the alpine zone.

The northern hardwood forest is home to a rich diversity of animals. The best times to spot birds and mammals are early and late in the day. Chipmunks, raccoons, white-footed mice, white-tailed deer, and porcupines breed here. Look for bears and moose, which are often seen on Katahdin. Listen for bird songs as you climb, especially in late spring. The red-eyed vireo is the most common bird of this forest, singing its *here I am, where are you?* song from the treetops. Hermit thrushes sing haunting woodland flute solos. Ground-nesting ovenbirds are more often heard than seen as they let loose their emphatic *teacher, teacher, teacher* outbursts. Scarlet tanagers and many colorful warblers contrast with the greens of the forest.

Amphibians still abound in Northeast forests, though some species have undergone drastic declines worldwide in recent years. The red-backed salamander is dark with a reddish midstripe, or all

Moose are at home in northern hardwood and spruce-fir forest zones. Watch for them along roads and beware! ▼

dark in the lead-backed form of the species. The red eft, the land form of the aquatic red-spotted newt, is bright orange, a warning coloration that alerts predators to its bad taste. After a hard rain, red efts are so numerous on the trails that you need to take care not to step on any. Also common are American toads, wood frogs with their black masks, and tiny spring peepers.

▲ Red-backed salamanders are common in the Northeast's northern hardwood forests.

As you ascend the mountain, the landscape changes. At or above 2,000 feet, the northern hardwood forest gives way to a transition forest zone. The Crawford Path, the Ammonoosuc Ravine Trail, and the trails from Pinkham Notch (see AMC's *White Mountain Guide)* all start in this zone. In the transition forest, spruce and fir trees intermix with sugar maple and other deciduous trees, although in the

Transition forest on Mount Adams ▼

past, spruce has been heavily logged at lower elevations. Higher up the mountains, spruce becomes the dominant conifer tree. As elevation increases, hemlocks and pines drop out, as do most of the deciduous trees. Of the major northern hardwood forest trees, yellow birch hangs in there the longest as you climb toward the spruce-fir forest zone.

The Spruce-Fir Forest Zone

Many environmental factors change at about 2,500 to 3,000 feet, and as you climb you notice the forest composition changing around you again. It is not the elevation itself but the changing climate that affects the forest. Temperatures are colder here, and thus the growing season is shorter. Precipitation is higher. Soils are wetter, more acidic, and less fertile than they are at lower elevations. Under these conditions, the evergreen conifers—especially red spruce and balsam fir—have an advantage over most deciduous trees.

Spruce-fir forest in Carter Notch ▼

▲ Prickly spruce (top) and "friendly" flat-needled balsam fir (above) are the two dominant trees of the spruce-fir forest zones in New England and New York.

Their needles conserve nutrients and can resume photosynthesis when temperatures are suitable. These two conifers can stand temperatures below –40°F, as can paper birch.

Red spruce and balsam fir are easy to identify: Balsam fir has flat, soft, "friendly" needles with two white racing stripes on their undersides. Balsam fir needles are often bluish green. Red spruce, on the other hand, is usually more yellow-green, with prickly needles whose cross sections reveal that they are square, rather than flat. Both species are shaped like Christmas trees, unlike shaggy, lower-elevation hemlocks.

When you arrive in the true spruce-fir zone, near 2,700 feet, paper birch is still present, as are striped maple, with green-and-white-striped bark and large "goose-foot" leaves, and mountain maple, with candle-like flower clusters. Mountain ash boasts white flowers in spring and bright orange berries in fall. It is a tree indicative of this zone and is found in open habitats along the trail. William Whitney Bailey, a Brown University professor, wrote of it, "This is the rowan of the Scotch and figures in many a legend. In late August and September its red berries are a striking feature of our mountain scenery."

Bunchberry, a close relative of the dogwood tree, has four lovely white bracts (leaf-like structures that resemble petals) and clusters of red berries later in the season. Other common spruce-fir zone plants include wood sorrel, with pink-striped white flowers and clover-like leaves; goldthread, with starry white flowers and three shiny evergreen leaflets; twisted stalk, with hanging, bell-shaped flowers; and waxy white ghost pipes, a true flowering plant that is dependent on tree roots and their fungi for nourishment. A special flower of the spruce-fir forest is the one that Carl Linnaeus, the 18th-century botanist who named plants and animals, chose for his namesake. *Linnaea borealis*, or twinflower, is a trailing elfin plant with twin tubular pink flowers.

Ghost pipes (below) and mountain ash (bottom) ▼

Canada mayflowers, bluebead lilies, and starflowers are still with you as you climb through the spruce-fir zone. As with many flowers that extend through the mountain forest zones, if you find them in bloom at the lower elevations, they may still be in bud as you travel higher. By climbing upward, you are walking back in time—you can enjoy the unique experience of revisiting spring in July at this elevation. In late summer and fall, tall large-leaved goldenrods and wood asters abound, as do many mushrooms, some of which are poisonous.

The spruce-fir forest has an emerald carpet of evergreen ferns, ground pines, and mosses. Big red-stem moss, *Pleurozium schreberi*, is glossy yellow-green, fern-shaped, and easily recognized with its conspicuous reddish stems. Clumps of dark green *Bazzania trilobata,* a large leafy liverwort, luxuriate here. Damp trailside banks are upholstered with bright green sphagnum, or peat, moss. Its special water-holding cells retain moisture even in dry weather. Upon reaching this zone on his way up Mount Lafayette in 1897, Bailey wrote: "The most striking feature of the vegetation is afforded by the billowy masses of moss that clothe the hillside, the rocks and the trees. These mosses are of infinite variety and beauty."

▲ Upper-mountain trailsides are often covered with a bright green peat moss.

The Balsam Fir Zone

By about 4,000 feet, red spruce drops out, and you continue climbing through almost pure balsam fir forests—the balsam fir zone. The physiology of this tree is adapted to high elevation. It is able to grow in the soils here, which are poor because decomposition is slower at lower temperatures and higher precipitation leaches nutrients from soil faster than at lower elevations.

It is even cooler, moister, and darker under the firs in this zone than in the spruce-fir zone. En route to climb Katahdin in 1847, Edward Everett Hale wrote about the "constantly changing brilliancy of these forests. I have called the color somber... not because of any darkness or dinginess of shade. The ground is a mass of moss, interspersed with flowers which our woods [in Massachusetts] know not... the fragrant Linnaea [twinflower] in all its profusion, oxalis [wood sorrel] as abundant as possible, and orchises."

Mosses and particularly their usually smaller relatives, the liverworts, do not need bright light and do best in moist environments. These plants are prevalent and occur in many forms in the balsam fir zone, creating an almost all-green zone. In a study comparing species diversity of plants in ecological zones in the Adirondacks, the ratio of mosses to flowering plants in the northern hardwood forest was almost equal. In the balsam fir zone, however, the number of different mosses and liverworts is much greater than the number of flowering plants. The liverwort *Bazzania* lives in this zone, too, forming large mounds, and many smaller species find their favorite microhabitats here. The shiny, braided-looking moss *Brotherella recurvans* is also an indicator species of the balsam fir forest. Mosses and liverworts, like fir trees, are evergreen and add their brighter shades of

▲ Old man's beard lichen clings to tree branches.

Mosses cover the forest floor in the balsam fir zone. ▼

green to the forest until the snow falls and again as soon as it melts.

Many of the other plants found in the spruce-fir zone are present here. So are many of the birds and animals. A number of warblers that migrate south in winter breed in the spruce-fir and balsam fir zones. Sometimes ten different warbler species can be heard on your hike from the transition zone to the balsam fir forest zone. Their bright colors flash through the forest. *Trees, trees, murmuring trees* sings the black-throated green warbler. Magnolia, blackpoll, and yellow-rumped warblers can be found here and up into the alpine areas. Golden-crowned kinglets call constantly but manage to stay out of sight. Brown-capped boreal chickadees have a different call (a northern accent?) from their black-capped relatives from lower down. Tiny winter wrens wind up for a seemingly impossibly long song, a rapid succession of warbles and trills. Swainson's and Bicknell's thrushes sing their beautiful fluting melodies. Two

▲ A tiny heart-leaved twayblade orchid, *Neottia cordata*, in the balsam fir forest

Gray bands of dead balsam firs alternate with young green fir trees, a phenomenon called fir waves. ▼

kinds of yellow-capped woodpeckers are found hammering away in this forest: the black-backed and the rarer three-toed species. Yellow-bellied flycatchers plaintively call *perwee* or *che-lek.* Spruce grouse can be spotted up here, bolder cousins of the shy, lowland ruffed grouse. Red squirrels chatter and scold you—this is their territory, not yours. They are fond of evergreen seeds, as are white-winged and red crossbills, which you may be lucky enough to see. A special treat is to discover a snowshoe hare in its white winter fur or a pine marten watching you from a tree.

▲ Pine martens are agile tree climbers. You may spot one in a balsam fir near treeline.

As you continue, you may pass through a solid stand of dead balsam firs—a natural fir wave. If you look over to other peaks while climbing, you will see this interesting phenomenon from a broader perspective—crescent-shaped bands of dead balsam firs, with declining mature forest on one flank and regenerating fir saplings on the other. The silver-gray bands you see in the distance consist of standing trees, "dead on their feet." Fir waves are a natural cyclic disturbance. On wind-exposed slopes, bands of dying trees move through mature fir forests, advancing about three feet per year. Where this phenomenon is well-developed, the bands are oriented in numerous rows. The average distance between two waves is about 200 feet and the repeat time 75 years or fewer. Fir waves can move up or downslope but always in the direction of the prevailing wind.

Fir waves have a significant ecological function. In his book *Nature Guide to the Northern Forest,* Peter

J. Marchand considers them an important means of cyclic rejuvenation in the White Mountain subalpine forests, too moist for renewal by fire and too cold for major insect outbreaks.

▲ Landslides and avalanches are common events on the steep slopes of Northeast peaks.

Landslides and avalanches are also naturally recurring events in this zone. Where the subalpine forest grows on steep slopes, the heavy weight of snow slips and sends an avalanche down the mountain. This happens repeatedly in Huntington and Tuckerman ravines and can be dangerous for spring skiers. Some of these avalanche tracks are bare; others are colonized by resilient mountain alder and other shrubby growth. Landslides, or "slides" to those who like to climb them, are also likely to stay open and visible from afar. Slides are especially conspicuous in the Adirondack High Peaks, especially on Mount Colden, where a 2025 slide buried the aptly named Avalanche Pass Trail under a massive pile of debris.

Into the Krummholz

The trees get shorter and the views get longer as you climb into the upper balsam fir zone. Here, the climate becomes about another three degrees colder between 3,000 and 4,000 feet. Fog is more common; precipitation is greater. In the White Mountains, the annual precipitation increases by about eight inches for each 1,000 feet of elevation gained. Trees are approaching the upper-elevation limit of their upright growth. The balsam fir forest becomes stunted; in some places it must be chopped through for trails. The trees can form a nearly impenetrable thicket, or tuckamore, the most difficult part of the ascent for the early climbers who had to bushwhack up the mountains (especially for women in long skirts!). This is probably the largest expanse of never-cut forest in the White Mountains, although there are pockets of beautiful old-growth forests lower down, like those at Gibbs Brook and Nancy Brook.

Beyond the stunted balsam forest is the krummholz (German for "crooked wood") zone composed of dwarfed trees, mainly balsam fir and black spruce. They often look like bonsai trees, but they have been shaped by natural forces, not human efforts. In the White Mountains and elsewhere in the Northeast, krummholz can be seen in the dwarfed balsam forest partially ringing the alpine zone and in island patches in favorable sites within the alpine zone itself.

Red spruce does not grow in the krummholz, but a related species, black spruce, does. Black spruce is a more blue-green color than red spruce and is

Krummholz trees are dwarfed and twisted into strange shapes largely by the extreme wind and the winter rime ice. ▼

▲ Black spruce high in the alpine zone is often a prostrate dwarf shrub or even a ground-hugging mat, sheltering from the wind.

remarkably adaptable. It grows far north in the subarctic, surviving where the permafrost only ever thaws to a foot below the surface. Black spruce is commonly found in lowland bogs but is found to 5,700 feet on the east, less-wind-exposed side of Mount Washington. In the alpine zone, it often forms prostrate mats, hugging the ground, avoiding the damaging winds. Its branches form roots when they press against moist ground so that even if its main trunk dies, it has the potential to form a new tree—a reproductive process called layering. Balsam fir also undergoes layering and is the more common of the two trees on the wind-exposed slopes, where clumps of gnarled krummholz extend up to 5,400 feet.

What causes the strange krummholz tree shapes—the flag, broomstick, and mop-head forms? Wind seems to be the main culprit. If you look at a small balsam fir sheltered behind a large rock, you will see that it is straight and tree-like until it grows beyond its protection. Then its windward branches

die, leaving green branches on only one side—a flag tree. You may see a whole forest of flag trees, signaling the prevailing wind direction, just below treeline. Strong winds often carry ice particles that kill tree branches in their path by scouring away needles and bark. A tree's leader branches may continually grow and die, forming a gnarled woody survivor, not a "tree-shaped" tree. If the terminal bud does survive, the tree may grow above the zone of ice abrasion and acquire a mop-head or broomstick shape.

▲ These "flag" trees indicate the direction of the prevailing wind—all the live branches are on the protected side away from the wind.

◀ Cross section of balsam fir from 5,000 feet on Mount Washington. Shown at actual size, the tight growth rings on the left indicate direction of prevailing wind. Rings show this to be 110 years old.

THE ALPINE ZONE

TREELINE SIGNALS the beginning of the alpine zone. Here is where upright trees end and alpine "lawn" begins, interspersed with only occasional krummholz. Every hiker notices this change—we welcome it for we have almost accomplished our long ascent to the summit. Alpine flowers await us as do, perhaps, magnificent views.

◄ Fall color on Mount Washington. Alpine plant life is often dominated by small shrubs, many with brilliant autumn foliage.

Treeline

Treeline has different causes in different parts of the world. In the Northeast, it has been formed in response to climate, not to human activities such as grazing or woodcutting. There are several climatic factors involved.

Wind is certainly part of the story; as described earlier, it is hard on upright trees. On cold, wet days it carries water droplets that crystallize onto trunks and branches, forming rime ice. You may admire these one-sided ice sculptures, but they damage trees and reduce their ability to make food through photosynthesis. Low temperatures also play a role in tree-growth limits but do not prevent the growth of at least some trees. Conifers survive temperatures down to –80°F in Alaska and Siberia!

▲ Rime ice forms on the windward side of trees, shrubs, rocks, and other upright objects.

Interestingly, treeline is not determined by the alpine zone's intense winter cold but is most highly correlated with its lack of summer heat, though other factors including high winds and thin soils are also important. The length of the warm growing season determines whether a tree has enough time to produce and harden new growth. If the frosts come too early, new tree shoots will die. A Mount Washington tree that can withstand a temperature of –50°F in January can have its new shoots damaged at 27°F in a late-August frost. The limit to tree growth in both the alpine zone and in the Arctic is close to the 54°F isotherm for the warmest month of the year, usually July in the northern hemisphere. (An isotherm is a line on a map where a particular average temperature occurs.)

▲ Rime ice can kill almost all their exposed branches, but krummholz trees carry on with new growth at their protected base.

Late snow cover can protect trees and be a boon to fast-growing snowbed plants, but it can also effectively shorten the growing season and prevent tree seedlings from becoming established.

Those Amazing Alpine Plants

Life in the alpine zone is hard, yet if you reach the Alpine Garden, Monroe Flats, or Bigelow Lawn in the Presidentials, Franconia Ridge, Mount Mansfield, Mount Marcy, or Katahdin in mid-June, you will see a dazzling display of flowers and plants that, in their variety and exuberance, seem to defy the extreme conditions.

No one who has witnessed this spring flower show can fail to be impressed by its beauty. For two weeks in June, the slopes are a pastel galaxy, the blossoms beyond counting. Perhaps the most handsome alpine plant is diapensia, which has dark evergreen leaves and waxy white blossoms spangling its compact form. The bearberry willow sports large, pink catkins that look too large for its prostrate stems and small leaves. Lapland rosebay explodes with showy magenta flowers alongside alpine azalea, whose starry pink blooms are a delight of color and form. With such an amazing array, spring flower pollinators are kept busy in the alpine gardens.

Sedges and grasses are major components of the above-treeline flora, although the alpine ones comprise relatively few of the hundreds of species of these groups native to the Northeast. *Carex bigelowii*, the sedge named for early botanist Jacob Bigelow, is one of the most successful, covering large areas of moist, exposed meadows. Some of the grasses and sedges also have lovely flowers—no petals but often

Bearberry willows are dioecious—plants are either male or female. These male catkins are bristling with pollen-covered anthers. ▼

colorful stamens, their anthers covered with golden pollen.

Many alpine plants do not have flowers at all. These are spore-bearing vascular plants such as ferns and clubmosses, which do have well-developed water- and food-conducting systems, unlike most mosses. In snowbed communities these may grow to six inches or, in the case of the mountain wood fern, over a foot in height. Other highly successful alpines are mosses and lichens. Mosses and liverworts flourish on rocks, in crannies, and in every rivulet. Lichens come in many colors ranging from gray to bright orange. They adorn every available surface: rocks, windblown ground, branches, and tiny twigs.

Mountain heath, *Phyllodoce caerulea,* is one of many members of the heath family found above treeline. ▼

Of the great variety of alpines, many are dwarf shrubs, some very dwarf. A good number are related—Lapland rosebay, alpine azalea, several blueberries and bilberries, alpine bearberry, mountain heath, moss plant, mountain cranberry, and small cranberry are all members of the heath family.

How do these alpine plants manage to flourish under extreme conditions? The watchword in the alpine zone is perennial—living more than one season. Whether a perennial plant is herbaceous (nonwoody), like mountain sandwort, or woody, like alpine azalea, part of the plant survives the winter, storing food for the following seasons. Annual plants, which go through their whole life cycle in one season, with only their seeds overwintering, just can't make it above treeline. The growing season is too short.

Lapland rosebay, *Rhododendron lapponicum,* blooming along Chandler Ridge on Mount Washington ►

Page 62: Mountain avens, harebells and false hellebore along an alpine streambed in the Alpine Garden

Herbaceous Plants

The following abbreviations and symbols are used in this section:

Plant Height in the Alpine Zone

<6" – up to 6 inches high
<12" – up to 12 inches high
>12" – over 12 inches high

Bloom Times in the Alpine Zone

❀ MAY – flowers in May
❀ JUN – flowers in June
❀ JUL – flowers in July
❀ AUG – flowers in August
❀ SEP – flowers in September

Northeast Alpine Distribution

▲ K – found on Katahdin
▲ W – found on Mount Washington
▲ M – found on Mount Mansfield
▲ A – found on Adirondack high peaks

Bluebead lily, *Clintonia borealis* · Found at all mountain elevations up to alpine snowbeds; smooth, shiny leaves; blue berries; also called Clintonia; named for 19th-century New York Governor DeWitt Clinton; Lily family

<12" ▲ K,W,M,A ❀ JUN–JUL

False hellebore, *Veratrum viride* · Common in low-elevation wetlands; also found in alpine streamsides and snowbeds; conspicuously tall among other alpine plants; stout stalk; cluster of yellow-green flowers; pleated, veined leaves; roots and leaves are poisonous; found in North America north to Quebec, south to Georgia; Bunchflower family

>12" ▲ W,M,K ❀ JUL–AUG

Rose twisted stalk, *Streptopus lanceolatus* · Found from hardwood forests to alpine snowbeds; pink flowers with red stripes, oval red berries; non-clasping leaves; found from Labrador to mountains of Georgia; forms a wine-red flowered hybrid, also found in the alpine zone, with the species below; Lily family

<12" ▲ W,M,K,A ❀ JUN–JUL

Clasping-leaved twisted stalk, *Streptopus amplexifolius* · Found from spruce-fir forests to alpine snowbeds; greenish-white flowers that hang under the stem-clasping leaves; oval red berries; found from Greenland to North Carolina and in eastern Asia; Lily family

<12" ▲ W,M,K,A ❀ JUL

Canada mayflower, *Maianthemum canadense* · Found at all mountain elevations, including protected alpine areas; 2–3 smooth leaves; fragrant flowers; ruby red berries; also called "false lily of the valley"; Butcher's broom family

>6" ▲ W,M,K,A ❀ JUN–JUL

Three-leaved false Solomon's seal, *Maianthemum trifolium* · Small, attractive plant found in both low-elevation bogs and in alpine snow-bed communities; it has only 3 leaves, thus the species is named "trifolium"; found from Labrador to Pennsylvania and also in Siberia; Lily family

<6" ▲ W,K ❀ JUL

Tall leafy white orchid, *Platanthera dilatata* · Found in moist areas, from subalpine forests and bogs to alpine ravines and streamsides; narrow leaves along stem; spike of spicy, fragrant spurred flowers; Orchid family

<12" ▲ W,M,K,A ❀ JUL–AUG

Mountain sorrel, *Oxyria digyna* · Found in alpine streamsides and ravines; kidney-shaped leaves; green-to-red flowers; also found in western U.S. mountains, Eurasia; Buckwheat family

<12" ▲ W,M,K ❀ JUL–AUG

Alpine bistort, *Bistorta vivipara* · Found in moist alpine areas; many tiny flowers on long stem; reproduces vegetatively by bulblets; also found in western United States, Arctic, and Eurasia; Buckwheat family

<12" ▲ W,M,K ❀ JUL

Mountain sandwort, *Mononeuria groenlandica* · Widely distributed in alpine zone; common along trails; a pioneer plant in disturbed areas; grows in tufts sometimes covering large areas; many 5-petaled flowers; blooms until frost; found in North America, north to Greenland, south to coastal Maine; Pink family

<6" ▲ W,M,K,A ❀ JUN–SEP

Boreal stitchwort, *Stellaria borealis* · Common in moist alpine areas up to Mount Washington summit; opposite leaves; weak stems; tiny flowers, also found in western North America and Arctic; Pink family

<12" ▲ W,M ❀ JUL–SEP

Moss campion, *Silene acaulis* · Dwarf alpine cushion plant; leaves are like coarse moss; 5-lobed, tubular showy flowers; taproot; also found in western and arctic North America, Eurasia; Pink family

<6" ▲ W ❀ JUN–JUL

Tall meadow rue, *Thalictrum pubescens* · A meadow plant found high up in alpine ravines; much cut compound leaves; clusters of white flowers that have no petals, but showy white stamens; grows to 6' tall in lowland meadows, but much shorter in the alpine zone; Buttercup family

>12" ▲ W,K ❀ JUL–AUG

Goldthread, *Coptis trifolia* · Found in all mountain zones; 3 shiny evergreen leaflets; single flower; bright-yellow rhizomes; found from Greenland to North Carolina, Asia; Buttercup family

<6" ▲ W,M,K,A ❀ JUN–JUL

Alpine bitter cress, *Cardamine bellidifolia* · Dwarf plant of alpine ravines; small oval leaves; 4-part white flowers; long, narrow seedpods; also found in Arctic, Eurasia; Mustard family

<6" ▲ W,K ❀ JUN–JUL

Alpine brook saxifrage, *Saxifraga rivularis* · Rare, found in alpine ravines, also near Lakes of the Clouds Hut and on Mount Washington summit; small leaves have 3–7 lobes; tiny 5-part white flowers; plant grows in tufts among boulders; Mount Washington is its southernmost site; also found in Arctic to Ellesmere Island, 82° N, and Eurasia; Saxifrage family

<6" ▲ W ❀ JUN–AUG

White mountain saxifrage, *Saxifraga paniculata* · Formerly *Saxifraga aizoon.* Rare alpine and boreal plant found on cliffs; easily identified by its lime-encrusted pores; white flower cluster at top of stem; also found in Vermont's Smugglers' Notch and the Arctic; Saxifrage family

<6" ▲ W ❀ JUL

Leafy stemmed saxifrage, *Micranthes foliolosa* · An arctic plant; once fairly common on Katahdin, now very rare; basal spatula-shaped leaves; most flowers replaced by leafy tufts; found on mossy rocks; Saxifrage family

<6" ▲ K ❀ JUL–AUG

Three-toothed cinquefoil, *Sibbaldia (Potentilla) tridentata* · Found on exposed ledges and rocky alpine habitats; 3-toothed evergreen leaflets turn bright red in fall; found south to Georgia, north to Greenland and Labrador; Rose family

<6" ▲ W,M,K,A ❀ JUN–SEP

Robbins' or dwarf cinquefoil, *Potentilla robbinsiana* · Very rare, found only on Mount Washington and the Franconia Range; listed as federally endangered until 2002, but now thriving (see p. 178); small leaves with deeply toothed leaflets; 5-petaled flowers ¼" across; named for James W. Robbins by William Oakes; Rose family

<6" ▲ W ❀ MAY–JUN

Mountain avens, *Geum peckii* · Found in alpine and subalpine streamsides, alpine snowbeds, and bogs; large, textured leaves turn crimson in fall; showy flowers on long stems; Rose family

<12" ▲ W ❀ JUN–AUG

It is hard to miss this beautiful flower if you hike the Alpine Garden Trail on Mount Washington from mid-June through July. You can see hundreds of blossoms at one time, especially in snowbed and streamside alpine communities. The plant, however, is actually very rare, found only in the White Mountains and on Digby Neck and Brier Island in Nova Scotia. Like Robbins' cinquefoil and Cutler's goldenrod, this flower is named for an early botanical explorer—in this case, William Dandridge Peck.

Purple avens, *Geum rivale* · A common lowland species, denizen of bogs and fens, that can be found in alpine ravines; relative of *Geum peckii,* similar but more cut leaves, and purple, nodding flowers; in eastern United States to West Virginia but also in the West and Eurasia; Rose family

<12" ▲ W,M,K ❀ JUL–AUG

Wood sorrel, *Oxalis montana* · A characteristic ground cover in the spruce-fir and fir forest, occasionally found above treeline; shamrock-like 3-parted leaves and candy-striped petals; leaves are tasty with oxalic acid; often grows with big red-stem moss; found Newfoundland to the Southern Appalachians; Oxalis family

<6" ▲ W,M,K,A ❀ JUL–AUG

American dog violet, *Viola labradorica* · An attractive flower with a conspicuous spur; white hairs ("beard") on two of the side petals; heart-shaped leaves on stems; found in lower elevation habitats, but at home in the alpine zone and in Labrador. The great-spurred violet, *V. selkirkii,* is rarer in the alpine zone; Violet family

<6" ▲ W,K ❀ JUN

Alpine marsh violet, *Viola palustris* · Found in alpine and subalpine ravines and streamsides; heart-shaped leaves; white-to-lavender flowers; found north to Newfoundland and in western United States; Violet family

<6" ▲ W,K ❀ JUN–JUL

Northern white violet, *Viola pallens* · Found in moist locations at all elevations, into the alpine zone; leaves are smooth, the flowers fragrant and under ½" long; the other common small white violet, *Viola blanda,* has two narrow petals, "rabbit ears," and is found in rich woods, not in upper elevations; Violet family

<6" ▲ W,M,K,A ❀ JUN–JUL

Fireweed, *Chamaenerion angustifolium* · Common lowland plant occasionally found above treeline; loose stalk of 4-petaled flowers; subarctic, found south to North Carolina mountains; Evening primrose family

>12" ▲ W,M,K ❀ JUL–AUG

Alpine willow-herb, *Epilobium hornemannii* · Found in alpine streamsides and ravines; opposite toothed leaves; pink flowers; long seedpods; found in arctic North America and Eurasia; Evening primrose family

<12" ▲ W,K ❀ JUL–AUG

Angelica, *Angelica atropurpurea* · Found in alpine ravines as well as at lower elevations; great size in lowlands, to 8', much shorter in the alpine zone; compound, much-divided leaves and smooth purple-tinged stems; flowers and fruits in large globular umbels; found Labrador to West Virginia; Parsley family

>12" ▲ W,K ❀ JUL

Bunchberry or dwarf cornel, *Chamaepericlymenun (Cornus) canadense* · Found at all mountain elevations; whorl of 4–6 leaves; four white petal-like bracts; inconspicuous greenish central flowers; scarlet berries in late summer; found across North America from New Mexico to West Virginia and Greenland to Alaska; also found in Asia; Dogwood family

<6" ▲ W,M,K,A ❀ JUN–JUL

Starflower, *Lysimachia (Trientalis) borealis* · Found at all mountain elevations; plants can be tiny in alpine zone; flowers have seven petals; borealis means "of the north"; found north to Labrador; Myrsine family
>6" ▲ W,M,K,A ❀ JUL–AUG

Alpine speedwell, *Veronica wormskjoldii* · Found in alpine ravines; stems and opposite leaves are hairy; blue flowers have four petals, two stamens; also found in western North America and from Greenland to Alaska; Figwort family
<12" ▲ W,K ❀ JUL–AUG

Pale painted cup, *Castilleja septentrionalis* · Found in moist alpine areas and ravines; tall, leafy spike; semiparasitic; related to western Indian paintbrushes; found north to Labrador; Broom-rape family
>12" ▲ W,K ❀ JUL–AUG

Oakes' eyebright, *Euphrasia oakesii* · Found in alpine zone only; small annual plant with round toothed leaves; semiparasitic on roots of other plants; tiny burgundy or white flowers; found north to Labrador; Broom-rape family

<6" ▲ W ❀ AUG–SEP

Alpine bluet, *Houstonia caerulea var. faxonorum* · White-flowered variety of the lowland species; found in alpine snowbeds and moist places above treeline; tiny opposite leaves; honey-scented 4-part flowers; found only in White Mountains and on the islands of St. Pierre and Miquelon; common bluet is sometimes found above treeline; Madder family

<6" ▲ W ❀ JUN–JUL

Twinflower, *Linnaea borealis* · Widespread and attractive trailing plant with small rounded leaves with a few teeth; very attractive twinned pink flowers; happy in the spruce-fir zone, found up to the krummholz; Linnaeus's favorite flower and named for him; found in most of the United States and Eurasia, but endangered in Connecticut; Honeysuckle family

<6" ▲ W,M,K,A ❀ JUL–SEP

Harebell or bluebell, *Campanula rotundifolia* · Found at lower elevations and in alpine zone, especially in snowbeds; only the basal leaves are round; the stem leaves are narrow; delicate stems support nodding bell-shaped flowers, usually a single blossom in the alpine zone; found north to Newfoundland, western North America, Alps, Asia; Bluebell family

<12" ▲ W,M,K ❀ JUL–SEP

Large-leaved goldenrod, *Solidago macrophylla* · Found in all mountain zones to alpine snowbeds; large broad leaves; ½" flower heads; found from Labrador south to New York and Mount Greylock; Composite family

>12" ▲ W,M,K,A ❀ JUL–AUG

Cutler's goldenrod, *Solidago leiocarpa* · Formerly *S. cutleri,* named for 18th-century botanist Manasseh Cutler; most common and smallest goldenrod in alpine zone; 2–7 leaves on stem; grows only above treeline from Maine to New York; Rand's goldenrod, *Solidago simplex* var. *monticola,* is occasionally found in alpine zone; Composite family

<12" ▲ W,M,K,A ❀ JUL–SEP

Sharp-leaved wood aster, *Eurybia (Aster) divaricata* · Common fall aster in woods to high on mountains; rather few heads, long white ray flowers; large toothed leaves taper at both ends; Newfoundland south to mountains of Georgia; Composite family

>12" ▲ W,M,K,A ❀ AUG–SEP

Purple-stemmed aster, *Symphyotrichum (Aster) puniceum* · Grows in wet soils at lower elevations, also alpine and subalpine stream banks and moist areas; hairy stems and leaves; flower heads surrounded by leafy bracts; found north to Labrador; Composite family

>12" ▲ W,M,K ❀ JUL–SEP

Alpine arctic cudweed, *Omalotheca (Gnaphilum) sativa* · A small, rare composite; less than 4" tall; gray-green with silky hairs and few flower heads; true arctic-alpine circumpolar plant; on Mount Washington, Katahdin, and Gaspé, but north to Labrador and Greenland; Composite family

<6" ▲ W,K ❀ JUN–SEP

Flat-topped aster, *Doellingeria umbellata* · A lowland species also found in subalpine ravines and wet areas; branching clusters of flowers; reproduces through underground rhizomes; Composite family

>12" ▲ W,K ❀ JUL–AUG

Arnica, *Arnica lanceolata* · Found in alpine ravines and on ravine headwalls; leaves and stems are hairy; leaves are variable; many 2" flower heads; found in North America north to Gaspé, west to the Colorado Rockies, California, and British Columbia; several other yellow-flowered arnica species are found in Rocky Mountains; Composite family

>12" ▲ W,K ❀ JUL–SEP

Three-leaved rattlesnake-root, *Nabalus (Prenanthes) trifoliolatus* · Found at all mountain elevations; variable 3-part leaves; in alpine zone it has dwarf form; Composite family

<12" ▲ W,K,M,A ❀ JUL–AUG

Boott's rattlesnake-root, *Nabalus (Prenanthes) boottii* · Strictly an alpine plant; triangular or heart-shaped leaves; named for its discoverer, John Wright Boott; found only on New England and Adirondack alpine summits; Composite family

<12" ▲ W,M,K,A ❀ JUL–AUG

Round-leaved sundew, *Drosera rotundifolia* · A carnivorous plant found in acidic wetlands, subalpine ravines, and alpine bogs; sticky "dew" on leaves traps and digests insects, supplementing nutrients for the plant; in the alpine zone, plants are much reduced in size; Sundew family

<6" ▲ W,K,A ❀ JUL–AUG

Trees and Shrubs

The following abbreviations and symbols are used in this section:

Plant Height in the Alpine Zone

<6" – up to 6 inches high

<12" – up to 12 inches high

>12" – over 12 inches high

Bloom Times in the Alpine Zone

❀ MAY – flowers in May

❀ JUN – flowers in June

❀ JUL – flowers in July

❀ AUG – flowers in August

❀ SEP – flowers in September

Northeast Alpine Distribution

▲ K – found on Katahdin

▲ W – found on Mount Washington

▲ M – found on Mount Mansfield

▲ A – found on Adirondack high peaks

Balsam fir, *Abies balsamea* · Found from transition into alpine zone as dwarf tree and mat former; erect cones; flat needles with white stripes below; also found from Labrador to Virginia; Pine family

>12" ▲ W,M,K,A

Black spruce, *Picea mariana* · Found in krummholz and prostrate mats in the alpine zone, also in lowland bogs; prickly needles; also found from Labrador and Alaska south to West Virginia; Pine family

>12" ▲ W,M,K,A

Larch, *Larix laricina* · Also called tamarack or hackmatack; common in lowland bogs and other northern wetlands but is also found in its dwarf or prostrate form in the alpine zone; turns bright yellow in the fall and then loses its needles—an unusual deciduous conifer; found north to Labrador

>12" ▲ W,A

Common juniper, *Juniperus communis var. depressa* · Found on rocky slopes at lower elevations and in its prostrate form in the alpine zone on Mount Washington and Katahdin; has sharp needles; modified cones look like blue berries

>12" ▲ W,K

Snowbed willow, *Salix herbacea*

Found in alpine zone only; tiny trailing shrub; round leaves; flowers in short catkins produced on separate male and female plants; fluffy seeds are dispersed by wind; once thought to be extirpated in the Adirondacks, but recently re-discovered there; the northernmost willow in the Arctic; also found in Greenland, Asia; Willow family

<6" ▲ W,K,A ❀ JUL–AUG

Bearberry willow, *Salix uva-ursi* · Found only in alpine zone, a prostrate dwarf tree with small toothed oval leaves, woody branches, and outsize catkins; often found growing in the shelter of an upright boulder; also found in arctic North America north to Greenland; Willow family
<6" ▲ W,M,K,A ❀ MAY–JUN

This species' scientific name comes from its resemblance to bearberry, —"ursa" meaning bear, as in the constellation Ursa Major. Bearberry willow and snowbed willow (see p. 81) are the only two truly dwarf willows you will find above treeline in the Northeast. It is one of six shrub willows that live in the alpine zone, all specialized for different habitats.

Willows have separate male and female plants, the males with showy pink catkins (middle photo), the females with maroon catkins in which the flowers develop into seedpods with fluffy seeds to be dispersed by the wind (bottom photo).

Willows all belong to the genus *Salix,* an early source of the painkiller salicylic acid used in aspirin.

Labrador willow, *Salix argyrocarpa* · Found in alpine ravines and moist areas; upright shrub; green leaves, impressed veins, silvery hairs beneath; silky capsules; also found north to Labrador; Willow family

>12" ▲ W ❀ JUN

Tea-leaved willow, *Salix planifolia* · Found in moist alpine areas, subalpine forests on Mount Mansfield; upright shrub; leaves whitish below; found north to Labrador and Alberta; Willow family

>12" ▲ W,M,K ❀ JUN

Heart-leaved paper birch, *Betula cordifolia* · Found in upper elevations, to alpine zone; heart-shaped leaves; reddish bark; found north to Labrador; Birch family

>12" ▲ W,M,K,A ❀ MAY–JUN

Dwarf or glandular birch, *Betula glandulosa* · Low shrub found only in the alpine zone; small rounded leaves with scalloped edges, abundant resin glands; in fall leaves turn a handsome deep red, found north to Labrador; Birch family

<12" ▲ W,M,K,A ❀ MAY–JUN

Small birch, *Betula minor* · Another shrubby birch, but not as small as glandular birch; leaves longer than broad with pointed leaf tips and rounded base; first collected by botanist Edward Tuckerman on Mount Washington in the 1830s; found from Labrador to New England and Adirondack Mountains; Birch family

>12" ▲ W,K,M,A ❀ JUN

Green alder, *Alnus alnobetula spp. crispa* · Found along streams in subalpine forests, alpine ravines; dwarf shrub in alpine zone; finely toothed leaves; found in Arctic north to Labrador, Alaska; Birch family

>12" ▲ W,M,K,A ❀ JUN–JUL

Skunk currant, *Ribes glandulosum* · Found at all elevations to alpine zone; low shrub; smooth stems; crushed leaves have skunk-like odor; red bristly berries; found north to Labrador; Gooseberry family

>12” ▲ W,M,K,A ❀ JUN–JUL

Black crowberry, *Empetrum nigrum* · Found in alpine zone and rocky lower summits; mat-forming shrub; tiny evergreen leaves; black berries; also found in Arctic, including Greenland; purple crowberry, *E. atropurpureum*, is also found in alpine zone, with purple berries and white fuzz on twigs; Heath family

<6” ▲ W,M,K,A ❀ MAY–JUN

Northern meadowsweet, *Spiraea alba* var. *latifolia* · Shrub found at all mountain elevations; alpine variety in alpine ravines and meadows; has short, compact flower heads; found south to Virginia, north to Labrador; Rose family

>12” ▲ W,M,K,A ❀ JUL–SEP

Dwarf raspberry, *Rubus pubescens* · Found at all elevations, in alpine ravines and meadows; trailing stem without prickles; white flowers; red berries; found north to Labrador, west to Colorado; Rose family

<12" ▲ W,M,K,A ❀ JUN–AUG

Bartram's shadbush, *Amelanchier bartramiana* · Found from subalpine forests to alpine zone; finely toothed leaves; unlike other shadbushes, this species has single flowers, or only a few in a cluster; purple berries are a favorite bird food; named for William Bartram, early American plant explorer; found south to Massachusetts, north to Labrador; Rose family

>12" ▲ W,M,K,A ❀ MAY–JUN

Mountain ash, *Sorbus americana* · Tree found in transition zone to alpine zone; compound leaves; white flower clusters; close relative *S. decora* blooms later and has somewhat shorter, broader and more rounded leaflets; found north to Greenland; Rose family

>12" ▲ W,M,K,A ❀ JUN–JUL

Cloudberry, *Rubus chamaemorus* · Found in alpine bogs in Presidentials and Mahoosucs; single white flower; ripe fruit is an tawny yellow color; found north to Greenland, Eurasia; Rose family

<12" ▲ W ❀ JUN–JUL

Creeping snowberry, *Gaultheria hispidula* · Found in spruce-fir zone, krummholz, into alpine areas; small evergreen leaves; tiny flowers; white berries; found north to Labrador, south to North Carolina; Heath family

<6" ▲ W,M,K,A ❀ JUN

Rhodora, *Rhododendron canadense* · Shrub found in bogs and up to alpine zone; downy deciduous blue-green leaves; flowers bloom before leaves unfold; found from Newfoundland to Pennsylvania; Heath family

>12" ▲ W,M,K ❀ MAY–JUN

Lapland rosebay, *Rhododendron lapponicum* · Found only in alpine zone; low prostrate shrub; magenta-purple (rarely white) flowers; evergreen, elliptical leaves with scurfy scales; dry seedpods; flowers at same time as alpine azalea and diapensia; found in Arctic south to Adirondacks and Wisconsin Dells; also in Eurasia, including Lapland; Heath family

<12" ▲ W,K,A ❀ MAY–JUL

Labrador tea, *Rhododendron (Ledum) groenlandicum* · Shrub found in bogs and at all elevations into alpine zone; thick evergreen leaves with orange-brown woolly hairs beneath, white on young leaves; found north to Labrador, Greenland, and Alaska; Heath family

>12" ▲ W,M,K,A ❀ JUN–JUL

Mountain heath, *Phyllodoce caerulea* · Found only in alpine zone, often in alpine snowbed communities; tiny, evergreen needle-like leaves; also found in Arctic, Eurasia; Heath family

<6" ▲ W,K ❀ JUN–JUL

Leatherleaf, *Chamaedaphne calyculata* · Shrub found in low-elevation bogs and in alpine zone; tough, leathery, scaly leaves; several varieties; found north to Labrador, Eurasia; Heath family

<12" ▲ W,M,K,A ❀ JUN

Bog laurel or pale laurel, *Kalmia polifolia* · Found in low-elevation bogs and moist alpine areas; green shiny leaves, white underneath; found south to New Jersey, north to Labrador, west to Oregon, Alaska; Heath family

<12" ▲ W,M,K,A ❀ JUN–JUL

Alpine azalea, *Kalmia (Loiseleuria) procumbens* · Found in alpine zone only; dwarf mat-forming shrub; ½" evergreen leaves; small red seed-pods; also found in Arctic to Greenland, Alaska, Eurasia; Heath family

<6" ▲ W,K,A ❀ MAY–JUL

Alpine bearberry, *Arctous alpina* · Found only in alpine zone; leaves are veined and textured, turn intense red in fall; flowers and thus berries are rare in the Northeast; food for people and animals, especially bears, in the Arctic; also found in Eurasia; Heath family

<6" ▲ W,K ❀ MAY–JUN

Bog bilberry or alpine blueberry, *Vaccinium uliginosum* · Found in many alpine communities; rounded, toothless, blue-green leaves turn purple in fall; blue fruit, often abundant; found south to Michigan, north to Ellesmere Island; Heath family

<12" ▲ W,M,K,A ❀ JUN–JUL

Dwarf bilberry or dwarf blueberry, *Vaccinium cespitosum* · Dwarf shrub found in alpine zone and on lower bare summits; toothed leaves are broadest above middle; blue berries; found north to Labrador; Heath family

<6" ▲ W,M,K,A ❀ JUN–AUG

Small cranberry, *Vaccinium oxycoccos* · Found in lowland and alpine bogs; creeping stems; small leaves; shooting star-like flowers; red berries; found north to Greenland, south to Virginia, Eurasia; Heath family

<6” ▲ W,M,K,A ❀ JUN–JUL

Mountain cranberry, *Vaccinium vitis-idaea ssp. minus* · Shrub found in alpine zone and on lower summits; mat-forming; red berries; also called lingonberry; found in Arctic, north to Greenland, Europe, eastern Asia; Heath family

<6” ▲ W,M,K ❀ JUN–JUL

Northern blueberry, *Vaccinium boreale* · a very dwarf alpine blueberry with tiny toothed leaves; sometimes confused with lowbush blueberry (below); Heath family

<6" ▲ W,M,K,A ❀ JUN–JUL

Lowbush blueberry, *Vaccinium angustifolium* · Found from lowlands to alpine zone; narrow, finely toothed leaves; found north to Labrador; Heath family

<12" ▲ W,M,K,A ❀ JUN–AUG

Moss plant, *Harrimanella (Cassiope) hypnoides* · Found in alpine snowbed communities; small, pointed evergreen leaves; *hypnoides* means "moss-like"; also found in Arctic, Greenland, Eurasia; Heath family

<6" ▲ W,K ❀ JUN–JUL

Mountain honeysuckle, *Lonicera villosa* · Shrub found in moist alpine areas, ravines; blunt leaves; paired flowers; twin berries; var. *villosa* is found north to Hudson Bay, south to New Hampshire; Honeysuckle family

>12" ▲ W,K ❀ JUN–JUL

Squashberry, *Viburnum edule* · Shrub found in moist places at all elevations; maple-like leaves; flowers in clusters; fruit is yellow, becoming orange and red; found north to Labrador, south to Pennsylvania, Asia; Elderberry family

>12" ▲ W,M,K,A ❀ JUN–JUL

Diapensia, *Diapensia lapponica* · Found in alpine zone, often in the most extreme wind-exposed sites; forms compact evergreen cushions; narrow spatulate leaves; waxy, white, 5-part flowers on short stalks; one of the earliest plants above treeline to bloom, often with alpine azalea and Lapland rosebay; found in Arctic to 82° N, Eurasia; Diapensia family

<6" ▲ W,M,K,A ❀ MAY–JUL

Clubmosses and Ferns

The following abbreviations and symbols are used in this section:

Northeast Alpine Distribution

▲ W – found on Mount Washington

▲ M – found on Mount Mansfield

▲ K – found on Katahdin

▲ A – found on Adirondack high peaks

Bristly clubmoss, *Spinulum annotinum* · Found in alpine zone; creeping stem; upright branches with spore cases on unstalked spikes (strobili) at their tips; *Spinulum canadense*, a similar clubmoss, has slightly shorter leaves

▲ W,M,K,A

Alaska clubmoss, *Diphasiastrum sitchense* · A very small clubmoss, an alpine species, often found near the tops of snowbed gullies; spore cases in unstalked strobili, plants less than 6" tall; compactly branched, seemingly without a main axis

▲ W,K

Fir clubmoss, *Huperzia appressa* · Found in alpine zone and on rocky peaks; small low tufts; spore cases at base of small evergreen leaves; often a pioneer plant on disturbed peaty soils in the alpine zone

▲ W,M,K,A

Ground pine, *Dendrolycopodium obscurum* · Found at all elevations into alpine zone; creeping stem; forked evergreen branches; upright cones

▲ W,M,K,A

Long beech fern, *Phegopteris connectilis* · Found at all elevations into alpine zone; variable size; triangular fronds; lower leaflets point down

▲ W,M,K,A

Mountain wood fern, *Dryopteris campyloptera* · Found at all elevations including alpine snowbed communities; broad fronds with toothy divisions

▲ W,M,K,A

Rock polypody, *Polypodium virginianum* · A very common fern at lower elevations, it is also found on the summit ridge of Mount Mansfield, in attractive clumps on boulders and rock ledges; evergreen, with twelve or more untoothed pinnae reaching the central stipe; Newfoundland south to Alabama

▲ M

Grasses, Sedges, and Rushes

The following abbreviations and symbols are used in this section:

Plant Height in the Alpine Zone

<6" – up to 6 inches high

<12" – up to 12 inches high

>12" – over 12 inches high

Northeast Alpine Distribution

▲ K – found on Katahdin

▲ W – found on Mount Washington

▲ M – found on Mount Mansfield

▲ A – found on Adirondack high peaks

Alpine sweet grass, *Anthoxanthum monticola* ssp. *monticola* (*Hierochloe alpina*) · Fragrant grass of the alpine zone; plants tufted; short leaves; florets with ¼" awns; found north of the Arctic Circle to Greenland and Ellesmere Island only to New York and New England

<12" ▲ W,K,A

Alpine timothy, *Phleum alpinum* · Found only in alpine zone; short cylindrical flower spike; found north to Greenland and in southern South America and South Georgia Island

<12" ▲ W,K

Spiked trisetum, *Trisetum spicatum* · Found in alpine zone; leafy stems; dense, spiky flower heads; curved awns; widely distributed in alpine and arctic habitats around the world

<12" ▲ W,M,K,A

Wavy hairgrass, *Avenella flexuosa* · Found at all elevations into alpine zone; hair-like leaves; florets have bent awns

<12" ▲ W,M,K,A

Canada reed grass or bluejoint, *Calamagrostis canadensis* · Found at lower elevations, alpine ravines, and alpine zone; large, purplish plume-like flower clusters; close relative of Pickering's reed grass, *C. pickeringii*, has fewer hairs below the floret; is also common in alpine sites, and only occurs south to the mountains of New England and New York

>12" ▲ W,M,K,A

Kentucky bluegrass, *Poa pratensis ssp. alpigena* · An attractive tall grass found in alpine zone; a non-native introduced from Europe

>12" ▲ W

Canada single-spike sedge, *Carex scirpoidea* · Found in alpine zone; unusual, separate male and female spikes

<12" ▲ W,M,K,A

Brownish sedge, *Carex brunnescens* · Found in all zones, frequent in alpine zone; small flower heads; brown or green

<12" ▲ W,M,K,A

Bigelow's sedge, *Carex bigelowii* · Forms large alpine meadows; dried-up leaf bases; dark purplish spikes; host plant for larva of endemic White Mountain butterfly; named for Jacob Bigelow, early White Mountain plant explorer

<12" ▲ W,M,K,A

Deer's-hair sedge, *Trichophorum cespitosum* · Important plant in alpine communities; dense tufts; turns tawny gold color in fall; can form uniform meadows above treeline like Bigelow's sedge

<12" ▲ W,M,K,A

Cotton sedge, *Eriophorum vaginatum* ssp. *spissum* · In bogs at all elevations; fluffy hairs on seed heads aid in wind dispersal; also called hare's-tail; abundant in Canada and Alaska

<12" ▲ W,M,K,A

Hair-like sedge, *Carex capillaris ssp. fuscidula* · Small delicate tussock sedge; grows in moist alpine areas; few small spikes on thin drooping stems

<6" ▲ W

Small-flowered wood rush, *Luzula parviflora* · Found at all elevations to alpine zone; broad basal leaves; many nodding flowers
<12" ▲ W,M,K,A

Spiked wood rush, *Luzula spicata* · Found in alpine lawns; large brown, nodding flower spikes; narrow basal leaves; circumpolar
<12" ▲ W,M,K,A

Highland or three-forked rush, *Oreojuncus trifidus* · A major component of alpine turfs; 2–3 leaves at top of stem surround spikes
<12" ▲ W,M,K,A

Mosses, Liverworts, and Lichens

MOSSES AND THEIR RELATIVES, the liverworts and hornworts, comprise the bryophytes, a group of nonflowering plants that ranges from the tropics to the Arctic and Antarctic. Mosses can take moisture and nutrients directly through their surface cells. This enables them to begin photosynthesis whenever the temperature is above freezing in any season, which gives them an advantage over most rooted plants. Some mosses and liverworts are found only in the alpine zone, not farther downslope. Some common temperate species, including several haircap mosses, do extremely well above treeline. Haircap mosses all have thickened, opaque leaves; several species have protective hair points at the ends of the leaves. Although most bryophytes are non-vascular plants, haircap mosses actually have a water-conducting system and can obtain water and nutrients from unfrozen soil. Some mosses look completely dried out and

There are places in the alpine zone where flowering plants can't grow, but a great many lichens and a few mosses find a home.▼

▲ Mosses can begin to photosynthesize at low temperatures, some even under a thin layer of snow.

dead in hot sun and drought but recover and begin to photosynthesize as soon as there is moisture. A good example is granite moss, *Andreaea,* which forms the small rounded black clumps on alpine rocks.

Mosses grow in a variety of habitats. Many live as hangers-on (epiphytes but not parasites) on living trees in the subalpine forest. In the alpine zone they grow in nearly all of the alpine communities but are most prevalent in the moister ones such as snowbeds, streamsides, and bogs. The big red-stem moss, a ground cover in the subalpine forests, finds a home above treeline in snowbed and other sheltered communities, as do other "feather" mosses. Peat mosses, *Sphagnum,* are ubiquitous in moist habitats. A number of Northeast alpine bog plants grow only in sphagnum moss. Several, though not all, of the alpine streamside and bog peat mosses make anthocyanins and other pigments when exposed to light and are various shades of pink, red, and brown. *Sphagnum girgensohnii* is green, genetically unable to make red pigments. It is the most common trailside plant in moist places below treeline.

Liverworts are so named because of their supposed resemblance in shape to livers and were once a sought-after cure for liver ailments. Most species do not in the least resemble livers but have stems with leaves. Unlike those of mosses, the leaves of liverworts are in two ranks so that the stems appear flattened. Even more than mosses, they prefer moist habitats such as streams and wet rock crevices. Most are small and inconspicuous plants, but there are exceptions. Three-lobed bazzania is a giant among leafy liverworts. It is conspicuous in large, dark green clumps in the subalpine fir forest. Many small liverwort species live in the alpine zone in varied habitats. One with hair-like or ciliate leaf segments, *Ptilidium ciliare,* lives in krummholz and alpine heath habitats.

In 2012, Jeffrey Duckett of London's Natural History Museum discovered the rare liverwort, Hooker's flapwort, *Haplomitrium hookeri*—perhaps the most ancient green plant to live successfully on land—on a cliff in Tuckerman Ravine. It had not been seen on Mount Washington since liverwort specialist Alexander Evans found it in 1917. It belongs to a 400-million-year-old group and lives symbiotically with an equally old fungus that probably enabled it to begin terrestrial life.

Lichens are extraordinary organisms. They are probably the best adapted and certainly the most diverse group in the alpine zone. Lichens are the result of a symbiotic relationship, almost certainly mutually beneficial, between a fungus and a green alga or cyanobacterium. In general, the fungus provides protection to the algal or cyanobacterial cells, and the latter provide photosynthates for the fungus, though that is an oversimplified description of the lichen symbiosis. Most important for our concerns, the lichen is far more durable in the alpine zone than

Lichens, some very old, are conspicuous in the alpine zone.▼

▲ Lichens on Katahdin's pink granite come in shades of yellow, orange, green, gray, brown, white, and black.

either of its components. Other fungi, such as mushrooms, do live on White Mountain summits, as do stream algae, but lichens are much more dominant and diverse. Like the mosses, they are able to absorb water directly and are adapted for photosynthesis at very low temperatures.

Moreover, lichens produce a great many chemical by-products, including pigments. Lichens add color to the alpine zones in all the Northeast mountains. They come in photogenic yellow, orange, rust, green, white, gray, black, and various shades of tan and brown. Lichens also produce an array of acids, which aid in breaking down their rock hosts. Lichens inhabit all of the major alpine plant communities. Some of those on Mount Washington are also found far to the north in subarctic and arctic Canada. On some Northeast summits, there are boulder fields where nothing is able to grow except a few moss species and a variety of lichens.

Lichen species come in several growth types: crustose (crust-like) lichens, which grow on rock, tree, and soil surfaces; foliose (leaf-like) lichens, very common on alpine soils; and upright fruticose (shrubby) lichens.

Big red peat moss, *Sphagnum* · Previously identified as *Sphagnum magellanicum,* has now been divided into several species; found in lowland and alpine bogs; large turgid peat moss with red pigment; grows worldwide

Small red peat moss, *Sphagnum rubellum* · Found in carpets in lowland and alpine bogs; a related species, domed peat moss, *S. capillifolium,* has raspberry-pink pompom-like heads close together, in hummocks

Girgensohn's peat moss, *Sphagnum girgensohnii* · This is the common green *Sphagnum* that forms carpets along trails up to the krummholz; star-shaped heads, long branches; named for an early bryologist from Estonia, Gustav Karl Girgensohn

Bog haircap moss, *Polytrichum strictum* · Common in alpine zone and lowland bogs; stiff, erect plants; gray threads on stem; angled capsules

Juniper haircap moss, *Polytrichum juniperinum* · This moss, like several close relatives in the alpine zone, has a hairy hood or calyptra covering the capsule; blue-green opaque leaves with smooth edges and angled capsules

Bristly haircap moss, *Polytrichum piliferum* · A small member of the haircap group, named for its white, hair-like awn ("bristle") at the leaf tip; in patches in dry open places in the alpine and lower elevations

Alpine haircap moss, *Polytrichastrum alpinum* · A large dark green haircap moss; opaque toothed leaves give starry appearance when wet and close up when dry; forms mats in alpine snowbed communities; long cylindrical capsules; common haircap moss, *Polytrichum commune,* is very similar, but has short, angled capsules and is found at all elevations

Blue-green pogonatum, *Pogonatum urnigerum* · Often found along alpine trails; broad-leaved rosettes; cylindrical non-angled capsules

Tree moss, *Climacium dendroides* · Large, distinctive tree-like moss found in wet forests at lower elevations and in alpine streamside communities; branch stems are red; long triangular leaves, toothed at tip; capsules are rare

Turf broom moss, *Dicranum elongatum* · This arctic moss forms compact tufts on Mount Washington; common broom moss is greener

Woolly shag moss, *Racomitrium lanuginosum* · Forms large hoary clumps or mats in the alpine zone; leaf tips have rough, toothed colorless hair points; *lanuginosum* refers to wool

Turgid bog moss, *Aulacomnium turgidum* · An arctic moss found on Mount Washington and Katahdin; overlapping leaves; resembles worms

Helmet moss, *Conostomum tetragonum* · Distinctive alpine moss with stiff and erect leaves in five ranks; up to 1" high, sometimes whitish-green, ovoid capsules; a good find on Mount Washington or Katahdin; also in the alpine zone on Adirondack high peaks

Shag moss (yellowish-green), *Bucklandiella (Racomitrium) microcarpos* · **Granite moss (reddish-black), *Andreaea rupestris*** · Both species grow on rock in the alpine; both are very desiccation tolerant; *Andreaea* has unique capsules that look like Chinese lanterns; shag moss has long-pointed leaves with short white tips; several species of shag moss grow in the alpine zone

Big red-stem moss, *Pleurozium schreberi* · The most common ground-covering moss in the balsam fir forest, but also found in protected alpine sites; the red stem is obvious when the moss is wet

Three-lobed bazzania, *Bazzania trilobata* · Large leafy liverwort; forms big clumps in subalpine forest; 3-toothed leaves in two ranks

Sickle moss, *Sanionia uncinata* · A forest moss also common in moist alpine habitats such as snowbeds; *uncinata* means hook or sickle, and several related sickle mosses live in very wet alpine sites; curled leaves have a costa or midrib, unlike leaves of brocade moss, *Hypnum imponens*, another curly forest moss found in protected sites in the alpine zone

Map lichen, *Rhizocarpon geographicum* · Very common crust lichen on rocks in the alpine zone; yellow-green color; "continent" patterns are formed by yellow-green or yellow areoles surrounded by a black margin

Rusty rock lichen, *Tremolecia atrata* · Common crust lichen on alpine rocks; named for its dull orange-red, rusty color; notice cracks and black edging; it has black, immersed apothecia, spore-producing structures of the fungus partner

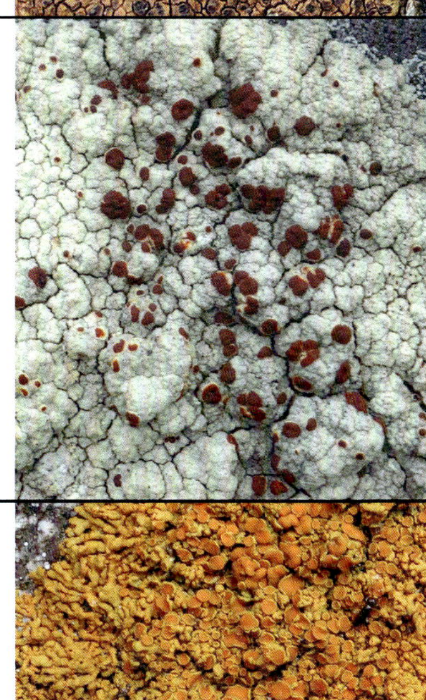

Alpine bloodspot lichen, *Ophioparma ventosa* · Striking alpine lichen; blood-red apothecia with cream rims the same color as the lichen; on rocks in full sun

Sunburst lichen, *Rusavskia (Xanthoria) elegans* · Found on rocks, human-built rock walls, and concrete; orange convex lobes radiate from the center of a rosette; a foliose lichen but tightly attached to the substrate; usually with deep orange apothecia; there are other orange or yellow-orange *Xanthoria* species

Target lichen, *Arctoparmelia centrifuga* · Foliose lichen that grows in concentric rings; recolonizes inner portions as center decays; species name refers to its growth from the center outward

Peppered rock tripe, *Umbilicaria deusta* · Up to 2" across with a rough-looking surface because of isidia, small asexual reproductive structures; several brown or black umbilicate lichens live on rock in the alpine zone, including blistered rock tripe, *U. hyperborea,* which has a convex surface with pushed up, wormy-looking ridges

Netted rock tripe, *Umbilicaria proboscidea* · Rock tripes attach to rock by a central cord; this one grows on alpine boulders; varies in size (up to 4") and color (grayish to brownish-black); always has ridges in the white crystal-covered center of upper surface; eaten by arctic musk ox

Foam lichen, *Stereocaulon* sp. · At least four species of *Stereocaulon* are found in the alpine zone, usually growing on rock, but *Stereocaulon alpinum* on moss or soil; difficult to identify, all are gray to white, covered with lobules somewhat resembling seafoam; common in the alpine zone on all our alpine summits

Worm lichen, *Thamnolia subuliformis* · Hollow, rounded unbranched or slightly branched stalks, 2"–6" long; worm-like; erect in clumps or often lying on the ground. This arctic lichen can be found on Mount Mansfield, Mount Washington, and Katahdin, as well as Adirondack peaks. It is rare on all of these except Mount Washington with its much more extensive and higher alpine area.

Freckled pelt lichen, *Peltigera aphthosa* · Large spectacular alpine lichen with both green and blue-green symbionts; the latter (the "freckles") are cyanobacteria which fix nitrogen for the lichen; also with black apothecia; underside dark in center without veins; found on wet soil in Alpine Garden on Mount Washington

Striped Iceland lichen, *Cetraria laevigata* · Tan or brown; broad lobes; white stripes along inrolled margins; crisp and brittle when dry; several similar brown Iceland lichens; this one very common under alpine shrubs like bog bilberry and other heaths

Reindeer lichens, *Cladonia stygia*/ *Cladonia rangiferina* · These two are hard to distinguish; in *C. stygia*, the cartilaginous layer at the base of the lichen is black; it is more common in the alpine; *C. rangiferina* is very common at lower elevations; has a brownish or dark gray basal area; both have less dense branching than *C. stellaris*

Alpine reindeer lichen, *Cladonia stellaris* · One of the most common and recognizable fruticose lichens; used for trees and bushes in architect models; found in alpine zone and other exposed areas; eaten by reindeer and by caribou in Quebec mountains; smaller and bushier than reindeer lichen above with tight heads to 2" wide and 2"–4" tall; star-like clusters at branch ends; circumpolar

Red-tipped goblet lichen, *Cladonia pleurota* · One of several lichens with red apothecia found in the alpine zone; cups short and stout; grainy soredia, or asexual reproductive structures; found on soil and rotting wood

British soldiers lichen, *Cladonia cristatella* · Named for the "red-coats" of the American Revolution; red apothecia are large and sit at the top of stalks (podetia) that are smooth, without soredia; found on soil, logs, and even tree bases; several other red-fruited relatives occur in the alpine; this is an eastern North American endemic species, not found elsewhere

Quill lichen, *Cladonia amaurocraea* · An alpine species; shiny, round stalks, 3"–6" tall, with pointed tips; frequently branching and with small flaring cups; New England mountains are its southernmost range

Rimmed camouflage lichen, *Melanelia hepatizon* · Circumglobal arctic and New England alpine foliose rock lichen; shiny brown lobes with raised edges; large brown apothecia with white lumps on their edges; underside black in center; *hepatizon* refers to the liver-colored lobes and apothecia

Snow lichen, *Foveolaria (Flavocetraria) nivalis* · Beautiful white or yellowish arctic lichen; fairly common on Mount Washington, scarce on other Northeast alpine peaks; lobes are flat with black dots on the divided edges; curled snow lichen, *Flavocetraria cucullata*, is similar, light yellow with edges curled inward, and prefers snowbed communities

Arctic saucer lichen, *Ochrolechia frigida* · The main body is a pale warty crust that grows on soil, moss and other vegetation; develops distinctive branched spines; saucer-shaped fruiting bodies are yellow or tan with white rims; circumpolar with disjunct populations in U.S. Rocky Mountains and Northeast alpine peaks

Fragile coral lichen, *Sphaerophorus fragilis* · This unusual lichen resembles a tiny coral or a coralline alga; branched, pinkish to mottled brown; found on rock on Mount Washington, Mount Madison, and Katahdin, but more common in the Arctic; another coral lichen, *S. globosus*, grows on trees in old-growth forests in Nova Scotia

Alpine mushroom lichen, Lichenomphalia alpina · An unusual lichen with a thin green algal crust; produces tiny mushroom-like reproductive structures that resemble chanterelles; found in arctic and alpine environments

Pink earth lichen, *Dibaeis baeomyces* · Unusual lichen with round pink apothecia that have definite stalks; sometimes covering large areas of the ground, often at lower elevations; similar candy lichen, *Icmadophila ericetorum,* is pale green with unstalked pink apothecia, and grows under krummholz on soil, moss, or rotted wood

Powdered sunshine lichen, *Vulpicida pinastri* · An easily identified foliose lichen found in the alpine zone on branches of dwarf trees; bright yellow soredia—the "powder"—are asexual reproductive structures easily seen on the edges of the lobes

ADAPTATIONS OF ALPINE PLANTS

TO SURVIVE in the alpine environment, plants capitalize on several adaptations. Small size is probably the most common characteristic of alpine plants. It is an advantage in keeping stems and especially buds out of the worst weather. It is also an energy saver: Small plants have to make less food to produce their leaves, flowers, fruit, and seeds. Some alpine flowering plants such as moss plant, *Harrimanella (Cassiope) hypnoides,* can go through their whole life cycle, producing flowers and fruit, while attaining only an inch in height.

Shape is important, too. Cushion-shaped plants have great advantages. Wind can flow over them as over an airplane wing. The dark, tightly packed evergreen leaves of diapensia absorb heat, creating temperatures inside a diapensia cushion that are higher than they would be in the frigid outside air, enhancing growth. Some cushion plants, such as moss campion, have central roots that anchor the cushion. These plants often put food reserves into their roots before their shoots; it may be ten years before a moss campion produces its striking pink flowers. There are other ways to stay close

Deer's-hair sedge has wind-pollinated flowers and a compact tufted form—advantages in tough alpine conditions.▼

▲ Woolly undersides of Labrador tea leaves protect the plant from winter damage and reduce water loss.

to the ground, where the climate, including both temperature and wind velocity, is less severe. Some plants form small or large mats. Others creep or sprawl, often rooting from the stems as they go, tacking the plant securely to the ground.

Hairs provide protection for some alpine plants. Where hairs grow on the undersides of leaves (as in Labrador tea, with its tawny wool), they protect the stomates, or leaf openings, through which gases are exchanged. Several mosses in the alpine region have leaves with hair points, sometimes making them look hoary, as in the gray green mats of woolly shag moss, *Racomitrium lanuginosum*.

Wind is a constant challenge for alpine plants. Narrow-leaved highland rush, deer's-hair sedge, and Bigelow's sedge, as well as many delicate-looking alpine grasses, bend with the mountain blasts. Their buds grow at or below ground level, so they can regrow if their blades are damaged.

Alpine plants often display striking leaf colors in autumn—blueberries, bilberries, three-toothed cinquefoil, and alpine bearberry turn shades of bold red and purple as a result of anthocyanins, the same pigments found in fall maple leaves and in apple skins. Many alpine plants have darkened leaves throughout the year. Anthocyanins absorb the higher levels of potentially damaging ultraviolet light found at these elevations.

Other aspects of alpine plant physiology are adaptive as well. Some alpines photosynthesize best at lower temperatures (55°F) than do lowland plants (70°F–80°F). Alpines begin growing and absorbing nutrients at temperatures hardly above 32°F; lichens and mosses do this at even lower temperatures, sometimes under a thin layer of snow. Lowland plants, however, may require temperatures of 40°F.

The spring-blooming alpine plants form their flower buds by the end of the previous season. Thus, they are ready to bloom by early June, even in mid-May if conditions permit, and the warmth they receive in late spring and summer is ample enough for plant growth, and for flower and seed development.

▲ Alpine bistort can reproduce vegetatively by forming bulblets along its stem—tiny new plants that fall and take root.

What about reproductive adaptations? Alpine plants have many strategies for successful asexual and sexual reproduction. Asexual reproduction is relatively more common in alpine plants as compared to their relatives downslope. Runners, bulblets, layering, and underground stems are all means by which alpine plants can provide their offshoots with larger amounts of food than they can provide to seeds. Three-toothed cinquefoil spreads by underground stems; some grasses and sedges form extensive turfs this way. Alpine bistort never produces seeds but is viviparous—the parent plant produces red bulblets on its stem, and these fall off to form new plants. Lichens and mosses can reproduce from pieces that break off, and fir clubmoss reproduces from small green, toothed flaps called *gemmae* as well as from sexual spores. All asexual methods produce clones—offspring with the same genetic makeup as the parent plant.

Sexual reproduction, whether it results in seeds or spores, has the advantage of genetic recombination, which may enable a species to survive changing climatic conditions. There is much flowering and seed production above treeline, and there are a surprising number of insect pollinators. Bog and dwarf bilberries, mountain cranberries, crowberries, and blueberries produce blooms throughout the early growing season. The resulting berries, so numerous and conspicuous in their summer and fall display, are eaten and disseminated by a variety of birds and other animals.

Most seeds germinate well, although some require a dormant period. The problem with sexual reproduction by seeds in the alpine zone is seedling establishment in a harsh, ever-changing environment. Alpines often have fast root growth, but of every hundred seedlings, frost heaving and soil movement kill all but a few in the difficult first year. Dispersal may not be very effective in the alpine zone either; in some experiments on Franconia Ridge, three feet from the parent was a long way for a seed to travel.

The alpine areas of our Northeast mountains are sometimes called "arctic-alpine" because a large proportion of the plants are also part of the Arctic

The flexible stems of sedges and rushes survive even in hurricane-force alpine winds.▼

flora. This is particularly true in the Presidential Range—almost two-thirds of Mount Washington's plants are also found in the Arctic. There are more than seven square miles of surface above timberline in the White Mountains—a large area in which these plants can find their own special niches. Plant communities in the Arctic and those above treeline in the northeastern mountains are much more similar to each other than either is to the alpine communities of western North America. this is partly due to climatic similarities (year-round humid conditions instead of intense summer sun and drought) and partly due to the continuity of migration routes between the Northeast mountains and the Canadian Arctic. You would see very few of our New York and New England alpine plants in the Rockies (or in the Alps), but many of them live in the circumpolar Arctic. Diapensia, highland rush, bog bilberry, mountain cranberry, and many others can be found in Greenland, Norway, Swedish Lapland, and Siberia.

Some plants found in lowland peatlands, like small cranberry, are also found above treeline, in alpine bogs.▼

Other plants found in the Northeast's alpine zones, however, are subalpine or boreal species that extend upward above treeline into favorable habitats such as streams, ravines, or protected late-lying snowbeds. Some, like Labrador tea, bog laurel, and small cranberry, are bog plants at lower elevations. In the alpine zone these plants are scaled down and have fewer, shorter branches and usually smaller leaves. They also have an accelerated growth cycle from the start of photosynthesis in spring to the production of flowers and fruit.

ALPINE PLANT COMMUNITIES

◄ Early blooming diapensia survives the harshest weather of any flower on the Northeast's alpine summits.

IF YOU ARE LOOKING for particular plants, it helps to recognize the habitats in which they are found. Plants generally live in communities where one or two species take up most of the room and use most of the resources. Other less-dominant species grow with or under them. A community is not a superorganism, but a group of plants (and usually animals, too), each of which is able to live within a particular set of habitat factors. Communities are quite variable. There may be a little more of one species and less of another, or an unusual species joining in as a result of changing environmental factors or chance occurrences. Where the environment, soil type, moisture level, or wind exposure changes abruptly, so do the communities. But more often, changes are gradual and communities intergrade, especially the various sedge, rush, and heath communities.

Each plant species has its own requirements and tolerances for temperature, soil, moisture, wind speed, and late snow cover. Some plants, like bog bilberries, are alpine generalists—members of a number of alpine communities. But some, like alpine bluets, are at home in a single community type only. You can become an

Honey-scented alpine bluets flourish in snowbeds on Mount Washington.▼

▲ Diapensia grows in wind-resistant mats amidst pink granite gravel on Katahdin.

expert in "reading" the landscape as you watch the communities and the environmental factors change together.

The alpine communities described below are named primarily by the plants found in each because they are the dominant organisms in each community. Moreover, plants are anchored and tend to stay in place. But mobile White Mountain butterflies, other insect pollinators, spiders, amphibians, and small mammals are present and important to these communities, too—and can be seen by careful watchers. Lawrence C. Bliss and Hinrich Harries both studied these alpine communities on Mount Washington in the early 1960s and gave some of them the names we still use today.

Diapensia Communities

Diapensia communities inhabit the windiest, most exposed sites, which are often ridges with little snow cover. Unlike most of the other communities, which have virtually solid plant cover, these may include patches of bare ground. Diapensia is characterized by its attractive, compact hummock shapes. In the severest sites, diapensia no longer forms hummocks but flattens out into a mat. Little blowouts occur where part of the plant has been gouged by the wind. Alpine azalea and Lapland rosebay also manage to survive such harsh conditions, thus forming a community of three of the most beautiful June-flowering dwarf shrubs. Bog bilberry and highland rush are found in diapensia communities, as is the later-blooming Cutler's goldenrod. Haircap moss and several lichens, especially Iceland lichen, grow here too.

Look for these communities on Bigelow Lawn, Monroe Flats, and the summits of Mounts Eisenhower and Franklin in the White Mountains, on the saddle on Katahdin, and north on adjoining Hamlin Peak. On Franconia Ridge, both Lapland rosebay and alpine azalea are absent from the diapensia communities. They do not occur on Mount Mansfield, and diapensia communities there are quite rare.

Bigelow's Sedge Meadow Communities

The most common community you will see on the upper slopes of Mount Washington looks like a grassy field but is actually a Bigelow's sedge meadow, kept moist by frequent exposure to fog and rain. Such a meadow can be seen on the northwest slope of Mount Washington, just below the summit. Little else grows in it, except mountain sandwort, which often seeds into disturbed areas along trails. Moisture-loving mosses

Bigelow's sedge meadows form where there is constant exposure to fog and rain.▼

look very green next to the tawny fall color and dark fruits of the sedge. Pure sedge meadows are absent on Franconia Ridge. They are very local on Katahdin, occurring in the vicinity of Thoreau and Caribou Springs in seepy soil, and in the Adirondacks.

Sedge/Dwarf Shrub/Heath Communities

▲ Tufts of deer's-hair sedge dominate this sedge/shrub/heath community, found on most of the Northeast's alpine peaks.

Another community type consists of a combination of more than 50 percent Bigelow's sedge with a variety of other species. This may be called the sedge/dwarf shrub/heath community and is found on the west and north slopes of Mounts Washington, Jefferson, and Adams and also on Franconia Ridge. Mountain sandwort and mountain cranberry are its two main associates. At one Franconia Ridge site, bog bilberry and three-toothed cinquefoil are part of this community. Reindeer lichen, Iceland lichen, and haircap moss grow here. In this community—which is consistently less moist than the snowbed or stream communities—lichens are more important in the ground cover than mosses.

Continuing down the west and north slopes of Mount Washington, highland rush, sometimes aptly called three-forked rush, becomes a prominent plant. In some places, such as above the Great Gulf, it seems to take over huge areas, looking like a field of windblown grain. Clumps of this rush appear in the sedge/rush/dwarf shrub/heath community, a large mouthful of a name, indicating a general mixture of plants rather than one dominant species. This community includes the turf-like Bigelow's sedge, mountain cranberry, and three-toothed cinquefoil. Look also for boreal bentgrass, a sparse but attractive companion plant. Lichens often abound here, sometimes providing as much cover as each of the major vascular plant species. Highland rush/Bigelow's sedge/mountain cranberry/lichen combinations are found high up on Boott Spur and at several sites on Franconia Ridge. A similar community of conspicuous highland rush occurs on Camel's Hump in the Green Mountains.

Dwarf Shrub/Heath/Rush Communities

A very common community in the Presidential Range has much less sedge and more highland rush and dwarf shrubs. It is the dwarf shrub/heath/rush community and covers much of the Alpine Garden and Bigelow Lawn. This community can be found on all the other peaks, usually within a few hundred feet of treeline. It is very species-rich—seventeen different vascular plant species, as well as many mosses and

Bluish bog bilberry and rust-tipped highland rush color this shrub/heath/rush community. ▼

▲ Mountain cranberry is one of many heath shrubs in the alpine zone, along with blueberry, bearberry, and bilberry.

lichens, may be found within it. Highland rush, mountain cranberry, three-toothed cinquefoil, and bog bilberry dominate, but diapensia, Bigelow's sedge, boreal bentgrass, Cutler's goldenrod, deer's-hair sedge, and mountain sandwort are also common. Rarer species, such as Boott's rattlesnake-root, can be found here, too.

On Franconia Ridge, this community contains large amounts of highland rush, mountain cranberry, reindeer lichen, Iceland lichen, and sometimes bog bilberry, as well as a significant percentage of Bigelow's sedge.

A very similar community also occurs on Mount Mansfield and Katahdin, where it has been called "alpine heath" by researchers Charles Cogbill and Don Hudson, and is widespread, especially among the rock polygons on the Tableland and around Hamlin Peak. It is dominated by bog bilberry and Iceland lichen, with highland rush, Bigelow's sedge, reindeer lichen, and alpine sweetgrass joining in.

Dwarf Shrub/Heath Communities

Dwarf shrub/heath communities do not have sedges or rushes as major components. Bog bilberry, mountain cranberry, Labrador tea, bunchberry, and lowbush blueberry are dominant. In the Presidentials, an average of thirteen different flowering plants are found in this community, and many of these are hard to find elsewhere. Dwarf shrub/heath communities can be found near the Alpine Garden, by Lakes of the Clouds, and on Mount Monroe.

Look for alpine sweetgrass and black crowberry, a dwarf, creeping heath-like plant with black berries and scallop-edged, dime-sized leaves. Crowberry is found near the Lakes of the Clouds together with bog laurel, Canada mayflower, and starflower. Watch for a tiny northern blueberry, *Vaccinium boreale,* with sharply toothed, very narrow leaves. Like other blueberries, it is handsome in its rich fall colors. Another interesting shrub, scarce on Mount Washington but common on Katahdin, is alpine bearberry, which has small, net-veined leaves and, in a very good summer, black berries.

The dwarf shrub/heath communities form dense mats, with crinkly brown Iceland lichen underneath the shrubs and almost no ground showing. Where there is winter-snow protection, bog bilberry is the dominant species, together with Iceland lichen. Franconia Ridge has dwarf shrub/heath communities in which bog bilberry and mountain cranberry are dominant. Similar communities with bog bilberry as the

In June, the clustered white blooms of Labrador tea stand out amid other alpine shrubs. ▼

dominant plant occur on Mounts Marcy and Mansfield, as well as Katahdin, often with some admixture of sedge or rush, making them hard to distinguish from the other communities described above.

Snowbed Communities

Snowbed communities occur where snow remains late in the spring, often into July. They are the most species-rich of all the alpine communities; more than 50 vascular plants, as well as many mosses, grow in them. Not only do these communities contain the most species, but 40 percent of the species sampled by ecologist Lawrence C. Bliss above treeline in the Presidential Range alpine zone were found only in this type of community. Some of these species are rare but others also occur in the subalpine forests, and a few of them even occur in deciduous forests. These species include Canada mayflower, goldthread, bluebead lily, bunchberry, and, most noticeably, the tall false hellebore.

Late-lying snow enables both boreal forest and rare alpine species to live in snowbed communities.▼

Dwarf bilberry is a dominant snowbed plant, as is lovely late-season hairgrass, *Avenella floxuosa*. The white-flowered alpine bluet is a variety restricted in Northeast to the White Mountain snowbed communities. This honey-scented flower is easy to find when it blooms in June. Dense snowbed communities at high elevations are also home to mountain wood fern, Bartram's shadbush, meadowsweet, twisted stalk, large-leaved goldenrod, and dwarf birches. Bigelow's sedge and bog bilberry become much more robust plants here than in their other habitats. Mosses and lichens are less prominent, but broom and feather mosses, more common in subalpine forests, occur in protected spots.

▲ False hellebore emerges quickly after the snow melts in snowbed communities and grows fast.

Other rare species are found where the snow lies relatively late. Two beauties are moss plant, *Harrimanella (Cassiope) hypnoides* (meaning "like a moss"), and mountain heath, *Phyllodoce*. Snowbed willow, *Salix herbacea,* is common high in the Great Gulf but scarce elsewhere. Thought to be extirpated in the Adirondacks, a new population was recently found. Mountain sorrel is found in the Great Gulf. It is a common snowbed plant in the Rocky Mountains, where snowbed communities are even larger and more diverse.

Extensive snowbed communities are found on the southeast and east slopes of the upper cone of Mount Washington adjacent to clumps of above-treeline krummholz. They can also be found in the lee of large rocks and in natural depressions. On

▲ Many plants from lower forest zones grow in snowbed communities; bluebead lily and bunchberry bloom here weeks after their lowland counterparts.

Franconia Ridge, ecologist Charles Cogbill, who studied all the vegetation there quantitatively, distinguished two types of snowbed communities: heath snowbeds and herbaceous snowbeds. One Franconia Ridge site on North Lafayette is considered a heath snowbed. Labrador tea is its dominant plant, with 60 percent of the cover; two other heath shrubs, mountain cranberry and bog bilberry, are also important. Bristly clubmoss and dwarf bilberry are part of that community as well.

Herbaceous snowbed communities on Franconia Ridge are more like those found in the Presidentials, with false hellebore, mountain wood fern, large-leaved goldenrod, bunchberry, dwarf bilberry, and mountain avens. Mountain avens is a nearly endemic species—it is found nowhere in the world except atop the White Mountains and on several small islands off the coast of Nova Scotia. A streamside as well as a snowbed plant on Mount Washington, it is a bold accent with its large leaves and yellow flowers in mid-summer, when the early profusion of spring blooms is gone.

Snowbed communities are also found on Katahdin, containing many of the same species, including dwarf bilberry, bog bilberry, hairgrass, glandular birch, moss plant, and mountain heath, as well as a variety of subalpine herbaceous plants. These communities differ from those on Mount Washington, containing more moss plant and mountain heath and lacking mountain avens, false hellebore, and alpine bluets. Katahdin snowbed communities are found under cornices where snow builds up or at the heads of steep gullies, and occasionally in depressions or on the lee side of krummholz patches. Mount Marcy has a late-lying snowbed below its summit, the "Snow Bowl, often visible in June from surrounding high peaks." There are no true snowbed communities on Mount Mansfield.

Streamside or rill communities retain moisture throughout the growing season and support a great variety of mosses.▼

Streamside or Rill Communities

Streamside communities abound in the Presidentials and contain many interesting plants. More than a third of the streamside species are restricted to these sites, as are many of the mosses found in and next to the water.

Look along the trail in the Alpine Garden. Streamside community sites can be seen right from the paths and are particularly noteworthy in summer as many streamside plants bloom later than the early heaths. Labrador willow, tea-leaved willow, and bearberry willow are abundant. All have conspicuous catkins, like the lowland pussy willow. Other streamside community flowers worth finding are mountain avens, harebell, alpine marsh violet, alpine willowherb, Boott's rattlesnake-root, and eyebright. Aquatic mosses, liverworts, and even macroscopic green algae grow right in the streams; peat, or sphagnum, moss borders them. Lichens are important in these communities, too.

Several unusual plants are found along streams and other wet areas, including pale painted cup, alpine bistort, spiked trisetum, mountain witchgrass, slender wheat grass, *Elymus trachycaulus,* and the attractive hair-like sedge, *Carex capillaris.* Distinctive-looking Canada single-spike sedge, *Carex scirpoidea,* grows here, in somewhat less-moist sites. This species was once dominant on Mount Lafayette but is now extirpated there. Two rare mosses, at home in the Arctic, occur here as well: a broom moss, *Dicranum elongatum,* and a large turgid moss, *Aulacom-*

Sustained moisture in streamside communities supports mountain avens, alpine violets, blue harebells, and other lovely flowers. ▼

nium turgidum, which resembles yellow worms.

On Mount Washington, some streams are actually springs that emerge at the base of the cone and flow out across the Alpine Garden. Many of their distinctive species are found in the Northeast only on Mount Washington, so please do not disturb them.

Alpine Bog Communities

Small alpine bog communities can be found south of Lakes of the Clouds on Mount Washington, on Mount Marcy, and on Mount Mansfield. Larger bog communities exist in the Presidentials, particularly along Crawford Path on the north side of Mount Franklin and south of Mount Eisenhower, as well as between Mizpah Spring Hut and Mount Jackson. Bogs are peatland communities, which are fed only by rainwater and are usually very acidic and low in nutrients. Bogs are underlain by sphagnum moss. Here there are several kinds, including two red species—

Bog communities with sphagnum moss and cranberries are found around small alpine lakes.▼

Sphagnum capillifolium, and *S. rubellum*—and brown *S. fuscum.* Small, or wrens-egg, cranberries creep over the moss, and white-tufted cotton sedge is the most conspicuous plant.

Bog laurel, also found in streamside and heath snowbeds, is present in these bog communities. Cloudberry, also called "baked apple berry" for the color of its fruit, occurs in the larger bogs along Crawford Path and in the Mahoosucs. The lovely mountain bog sedge, *Carex paupercula,* grows in small clumps on the edges of alpine bogs that surround small lakes in the alpine zone.

▲ Alpine ravine communities contain species, like alpine speedwell and arnica, not found elsewhere in the alpine zone.

Alpine Ravine Communities

This community is a special type of snowbed that occurs in the upper parts of major ravines where huge amounts of snow collect in winter and persist in spring. Tuckerman and Huntington ravines, Oakes Gulf, and the Great Gulf are the most notable ravines on Mount Washington, and Katahdin's most notable ravines are the North and South Basins. These features have bowl-shaped headwalls rimmed by alpine cliffs cut by avalanche gullies and rill streams. Many rare plants thrive in this habitat. Conditions are similar to those in the higher-elevation snowbed and rill communities, with late snowmelt dates and perpetual moisture in the growing season.

Tea-leaved and Labrador willows, green alder, and dwarf bilberry are characteristic ravine shrubs, along with alpine meadowsweet. The tiny, snowbed

▲ Steep-sided ravines collect huge amounts of snow that last into late spring.

willow can be found on the headwalls of Tuckerman Ravine and the Great Gulf on Mount Washington, on Katahdin, with a small population in the Adirondacks. It requires a winter snow cover and is an abundant snowbed plant in the Arctic.

Special herbaceous plants to look for include mountain sorrel, alpine marsh violet, alpine willow herb, and arnica, with its cheerful yellow blooms. Flowering spikes of tall white orchids bloom in July. Also growing here is pale painted cup, a subalpine and alpine plant found in three Mount Washington ravines, but hard to find elsewhere. Lovely blue-flowered alpine speedwell is found along streams in Tuckerman Ravine and on the peaty ledges of Huntington Ravine and the Great Gulf.

A variety of moss and liverwort species, some of them rare, also grow in this community. These ravines are challenging to climb (or ski!) and rewarding to sharp-eyed botanizers.

Birds

MANY INTERESTING BIRDS live below treeline in the spruce-fir and balsam fir forests. Do not miss the chance to do some bird-watching (and listening) on your way up the mountain.

There are birds to be found on the summits as well. Gray jays will greet you—and probably try to steal your sandwiches, too. Crows are not generally found at these elevations, but acrobatic ravens will soar, tumble, and give their coarse croaking call. Ravens nest on Mount Mansfield on the cliffs northeast of the Chin. Juncos, with their round forms and conspicuous white tail feathers, commonly nest in the alpine zone. Their song is a continuous trill that sounds like a musical sewing machine. Also breeding in the alpine zone are white-throated sparrows. The male has brighter white stripes and a yellow spot in the breeding plumage near the eye. He may seek you out and answer your whistle if you imitate his clear *old Sam Peabody, Peabody* call.

▲ White-throated sparrows sing from the tops of the krummholz trees.

Black-and-white-striped blackpolls and yellow-rumped warblers are sometimes found above treeline, though they usually nest in the subalpine forest trees. A pair of yellow-rumped warblers was found nesting in one of the small bogs on Mount Mansfield. Bicknell's thrushes are seen regularly in the alpine zone on Mount Mansfield and nest in the subalpine forest, as do boreal chickadees and golden-crowned kinglets. These birds are found in the Adirondacks, Presidentials, and on Katahdin as well.

▲ A female spruce grouse in krummholz zone which provides her diet of spruce and fir needles.

American pipits, brown birds with long legs and white tail feathers, can be seen on all the New England alpine summits, especially in the fall, during their migration south from breeding grounds in the Arctic tundra. Pipits nest on Katahdin and Mount Washington. On calm July days, lucky hikers may see and hear the males' courtship flights over the Alpine Garden and Great Gulf.

Ground-nesting juncos breed in krummholz and alpine areas.▼

Dark-eyed junco, *Junco hyemalis* · Sings and breeds on all Northeast summits; slate gray; round bird with white belly; white outer tail feathers; trilling song, like a musical sewing machine; 6"

Common raven, *Corvus corax* · Unmistakable raucous black bird; heavy bill; wedge-shaped tail; shaggy throat feathers; distinctive croak; watch for aerial acrobatics; in alpine and lower zones; 24"

Gray jay or Canada jay, *Perisoreus canadensis* · Gray-backed, white below; juveniles are sooty; widespread in North America; Northeast subspecies has white forehead, brownish crown; not shy; 12"

American pipit, *Anthus rubescens* · Brown-streaked ground bird; slender bill; white tail feathers; pumps tail up and down as it walks; fall visitor to New England summits; breeds on Katahdin; 6"–7"

If you climb to the top of Katahdin, its neighbor Mount Hamlin, or Mount Washington, you may be able to see and hear one of New England's rare birds, the American pipit. Small and brown, with a thin bill and white tail feathers, it bobs its tail as it feeds on spiders and insects. Pipits breed on these mountains, in the Chic-Chocs of Quebec's Gaspé Peninsula, and in the American Arctic, Alaska, and the Rocky Mountains. They nest in a sheltered place on the ground, laying 5–7 eggs. The photo below shows fledglings in nest on Mount Washington. Pipits are one of the few birds you will hear sing on the New England summits. The 2-note flight call sounds like *pip-et*, the source of its name. In mid-June, on calm, clear days, you may see males perform dramatic territorial displays—flying upward then swooping down while singing a rapid series of notes. Pipits are migratory birds and winter across the southern United States and Mexico.

Spruce grouse, *Canachites canadensis* · Brown, chicken-size ground bird; perches in trees; male has dark throat, red eye comb; found in spruce-fir and fir forests; tamer than ruffed grouse; 16"

White-throated sparrow, *Zonotrichia albicollis* · White throat; distinctive black-and-white crown; breeding male has yellow "eyebrow"; breeds in all New York and New England alpine areas; whistles *old Sam Peabody, Peabody;* one of the few birds that actually nests in the alpine zone, others include the junco and occasionally yellow-rumped and blackpoll warblers; nests are built on or close to the ground and lined with fine grass; female lays pale blue or blue-green eggs with dark speckles; 7"

Boreal chickadee, *Poecile hudsonicus* · Similar to black-capped chickadee but with a brown cap and slower, more nasal call; breeds in subalpine forests and north to Hudson Bay and Alaska; 5"

Red crossbill, *Loxia curvirostra* · This bird and white-winged crossbill, *L. leucoptera* (6½"), have unique crossed bill tips used to extract conifer seeds; females are drab olive; males are brick red; 8½"

White-winged crossbill, *Loxia leucoptera* · Striking bird with bill adapted for extracting conifer seeds from cones; rosy-colored male has black and white wings; female is yellow-green; found in balsam fir forests and above in the New England and Adirondack mountains, or sometimes lower if cone crop is poor; 6"–6½"

Blackpoll warbler, *Setophaga striata* · Streaked with black and white, black cap, white cheeks; sings a high *zi, zi, zi;* nests in conifers near treeline; breeds north to Alaska; winters in South America; 5"

Magnolia warbler, *Setophaga magnolia* · Usually found in conifer forests, sometimes to treeline; yellow breast with dark streaks; clear whistled song; winters in Caribbean and Central America; 5"

Yellow-rumped warbler, *Setophaga coronata* · Warbler most likely to be seen in the alpine zone; yellow throat, side, cap, and rump; slender; narrow bill; an insect eater; lines nest with many feathers; 5"

Black-throated green warbler, *Setophaga virens* · Strikingly colored with yellow face; sings *trees, trees, murmuring trees;* hawks insects on the wing and forages in spruce and fir trees; found along upper trails on all Northeast mountains; breeds in conifer forests of the Northeast and Canada, but winters in Mexico, the Caribbean, and Ecuador; 5"

Black-throated blue warbler, *Setophaga caerulescens* · Wood warbler and forest dweller, formerly of the genus *Dendroica* but like all warblers in this book, recently had its genus changed after DNA studies; breeds in the Southern Appalachians as well as in the northeastern forests; nests in shrubs near the ground; 5"

Pine siskin, *Spinus pinus* · Small, brown, and striped, but the males often flash bright yellow wing markings; found breeding in alpine zones of Northeast mountains, and also in the Rockies and Canada, but they are nomadic, respond to mountain seed crops, and may appear well below mountains in winter; 4½"–5"

Golden-crowned kinglet, *Regulus satrapa* · Tiny round bird; common up to treeline; easily heard but hard to see; breeds in conifer forests in New York and New England; 4"

Ruby-crowned kinglet, *Corthylio calendula* · Tiny round bird; common up to treeline; easily heard but hard to see; breeds in lower-elevation conifer forests in New York and New England; 4"

Black-backed woodpecker, *Picoides arcticus* · Two rare northern woodpeckers with yellow on their heads are found in Northeastern subalpine forests; the rarer three-toed woodpecker, *P. tridactylus,* has a barred back; 12"

Winter wren, *Troglodytes hiemalis* · Tiny bird with stubby cocked tail; very long, beautiful song; sometimes seen at treeline; nests in conifer forests north and west to Alaska, winters in southern United States; 4"

Bicknell's thrush, *Catharus bicknelli* · A fairly recently recognized species separated from the gray-cheeked thrush; endangered and currently under study; breeds in the Catskill and Adirondack mountains, Mount Mansfield, and Mount Washington; related to Swainson's and hermit thrushes; 8"

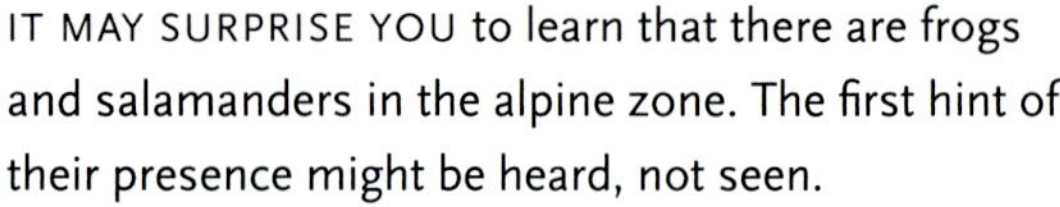

Amphibians

IT MAY SURPRISE YOU to learn that there are frogs and salamanders in the alpine zone. The first hint of their presence might be heard, not seen.

Beginning early in June at Mount Washington's Lakes of the Clouds, you may hear hardy wood frogs calling, a croaking chuckle. As soon as the temperature reaches 40°F, spring peepers sing their high-pitched notes with an occasional trill. The American toad deposits its string of eggs in small ephemeral pools that dry up later in the season. Listen for its long single-note trill. You can find red efts, the early land stage of the red-spotted newt, and perhaps the green frog in the alpine zone, but the latter breeds at lower elevations. Look for amphibian eggs and tadpoles in Lakes of the Clouds and in Star Lake, below Mount Madison.

Spring peeper in Huntington Ravine at 4,500 feet (below) and wood frog egg masses at 5,200 feet on Mount Washington (bottom) ▼

Where do these animals spend winter? Toads, wood frogs, and spring peepers may hibernate below treeline in subzero weather and migrate to the alpine ponds in spring.

▲ Red-spotted newts are found in Lakes of the Clouds—gilled larva underwater (top), female, fat with eggs, and male (above).

Mount Mansfield has its own Lake of the Clouds, but it is subalpine at 3,900 feet. Amphibians have been studied here, too—the same species that breed in Mount Washington's lakes above 5,000 feet—as well as spotted, northern dusky, and northern two-lined salamanders: seven species in all.

On Katahdin, amphibians breed in subalpine Chimney Pond and other high-elevation ponds and streams. Wood frogs, American toads, and spotted and northern two-lined salamanders were photographed on Katahdin by Charley Eiseman, Mike Jones, and Liz Willey, respectively, and published in Jones and Willey's *Eastern Alpine Guide* (New Salem, MA: Beyond Ktaadin and Boghaunter Books, 2012).

Green frog, *Lithobates clamitans* · Bright green, can also be greenish-brown, yellow-green, or even (rarely) blue; male has bright yellow throat and very large eardrums; female lays up to 7,000 eggs in single mass; most tadpoles overwinter before maturing; highest breeding site at Mount Washington's Hermit Lake, but adults have been recorded in the alpine zone; 3"–5"

Spring peeper, *Pseudacris crucifer* · Small tree frog; nocturnal and mostly terrestrial; brown coloring varies, but always with an X on its back; lays eggs in the water on twigs or aquatic plants; in low-elevation wetlands, its nightly chorus is an early sign of spring; in the alpine zone, it breeds in mid-June and July in the Lakes of the Clouds, Star Lake, and other open water sources; 1½"

American toad, *Anaxyrus americanus* · Common terrestrial eastern toad; usually brown with spots containing one, sometimes two warts, but color can change with temperature, humidity, or stress; the only toad that lives in the Northeast's spruce-fir forest and alpine zones; breeds in Chimney Pond on Katahdin; females lay up to 20 eggs in long strings; 2"–4"

Wood frog, *Lithobates sylvaticus* · Hibernates under leaf litter; survives severe cold by producing an antifreeze; some of its tissues may actually freeze; female attaches egg masses to underwater vegetation (below); first amphibian to arrive at Lakes of the Clouds to breed in spring; also breeds on Chimney Pond on Katahdin; the only frog found north of the Arctic Circle; 2"–3"

Spotted salamander, *Amblystoma maculatum* · A large salamander with irregular rows of yellow spots; belongs to a group called mole salamanders; spends much of its time underground, migrates to vernal pools and ponds to breed; occurs widely in the subalpine areas of New England and lay its eggs in Chimney Pond on Katahdin; 5"–9"

Red-spotted newt, *Notophthalmus viridescens* · Lays eggs on aquatic plants; tadpoles mature into terrestrial red eft juveniles (top) commonly seen in lower elevation forests; eft returns to water after 2–3 years; aquatic adult (right) is olive green with red spots; rare in the alpine zone, it has been recorded in Lakes of the Clouds on Mount Washington; 2¾"–4¾"

Northern two-lined salamander, *Eurycea bislineata* · A small slender salamander with two black stripes; prefers cool rocky streams and seeps; common in the Northeast's mountains and beyond to northern Quebec; this species has an elaborate courtship; the female finds a suitable nest site and guards her eggs until they hatch; known to breed in high-elevation wetlands on Katahdin; 2½"–4¾"

Mammals

MAMMALS ARE RELATIVELY RARE on the Northeast's alpine summits. Some species, however, are easily seen on your way up the mountains. Red squirrels are at home in the spruce-fir and fir forests. They are active during the day and throughout the year, and eat a variety of fruits, nuts, conifer seeds, eggs, and fungi. The red squirrel is thus part of many food chains and is itself eaten by martens and other predators.

▲ A red squirrel, just below the summit of Mount Washington.

Moose may also be seen during your climbs, particularly on Katahdin. There, the moose, including cows with calves, tend to stay around ponds and wetlands in the summer, eating aquatic vegetation. In the fall, they move up the mountain, even high up on the Appalachian Trail, and browse in or near the krummholz on twigs, bark, and perhaps lichens. Moose occasionally traverse the White Mountain summits as well. They are big, powerful animals, and may look awkward, but they can swim as fast as two people can paddle a canoe and are able to run up to 35 mph on land. Beware of moose on highways at night—in New Hampshire and Maine, motorists on mountain roads are more likely to be killed by moose than by drunk drivers.

▲ Porcupines are often seen in forests below, but it's exciting to find one in the krummholz, or even in the alpine zone.

Two mammals you are most likely to see above treeline are snowshoe hares and, high on Mount Washington, woodchucks! Woodchucks belong to the same genus as the whistling marmots of the western mountains. We don't expect to find them far from vegetable gardens, but like snowshoe hares, they have a wide range, from Hudson Bay in the East to Alaska in the West. Woodchucks are actually beneficial in wild areas because they dig burrows that later become homes for other animals. They are largely diurnal animals and eat a variety of plants. They hibernate for about five months of the year (longer above treeline), but you may see them feeding or hear them whistle near their burrows on a summer day in the Alpine Garden.

▲ Snowshoe hares gradually turn from summer brown to winter white to match the landscape.

Snowshoe hares are commonly found on all the Northeast's mountains. You may not see these largely nocturnal animals in the alpine zone unless you stay overnight at one of AMC's high huts. You're more likely to see signs a snowshoe hare has left behind—bitten-off twigs of alpine shrubs or pellet-like droppings. They are comparable in size to eastern cottontails, which do not occur on the high peaks. Snowshoe hares sometimes defend territories during the breeding season but at other times may wander up to one mile. There are many dangers in a snowshoe hare's life, especially in the alpine zone, and they rarely live longer than three years in the wild.

Snowshoe hares are dark brown in summer and turn camouflage white in winter, the key to their second common name: varying hare. This type of seasonal color change has evolved in many animals, including ermines and ptarmigans. Interestingly, our hare's northern cousin, the Arctic hare, remains all-white all year in the northern Arctic, but its color does vary in its lower range, as in the mountains of Newfoundland. Look for snowshoe hare tracks. Its large hind feet—which prevent it from sinking into the snow—are the "snowshoes" of its name. The fur on their soles also protects their feet from freezing. These hares feed on many types of food. They can be partly carnivorous and may eat dead mice or other rodents. In winter, snowshoe hares must survive on twigs, bark, and buds; in summer, they feed on a variety of vegetation. In addition to their other challenges, the "amazing alpine plants" must cope with hungry herbivores!

Other animals have been sighted or trapped in the alpine zone. Bobcats, lynx, coyotes, and foxes are visitors here, as are members of the carnivorous weasel family. Short-tailed weasels have been seen by the authors in the Alpine Garden. Like snowshoe hares, they turn pure white in winter. American martens range from New York, New England, and Eastern Canada to the Rockies and Alaska. Their yellowish-brown fur is distinctive. Martens spend much of their time in trees but also forage on the ground. They are largely carnivorous, feeding on red squirrels and other small

The red fox is an efficient predator and hunts high in the alpine zone. ▼

▲ Hikers may see a curious short-tailed weasel watching from the cover of rocks or krummholz trees. In winter, this predator changes color to blend with snow.

animals as well as birds, insects, and even fruits and nuts. They den in trees or logs, and may range as far as 15 miles, traveling at least occasionally into the alpine zone. Their scat is found along all the major trails on Mount Washington. Martens and their larger relatives, fishers, have both been observed along the trails up Katahdin. Fishers have dark brown coats with white-tipped hairs. They were once more common in our mountain forests but were nearly trapped out of existence because their beautiful fur was highly desired. Like martens, they are also mainly carnivorous and are one of the few predators that feed on porcupines.

Carnivorous shrews must catch and eat food equivalent to their own weight every day, year-round. It is hard to see how they can survive on our mountain summits, but several species have been trapped above timberline. These include smoky shrews and short-tailed shrews, which have poisonous saliva used to paralyze prey. Pygmy shrews of mountain slope forests are probably the smallest living mammals, each weighing no more than a dime. Pygmy shrews have been found on Mount Marcy and Mount Mansfield; their habits await further study. The rare long-tailed shrew has been trapped in Tuckerman Ravine.

▲ Short-tailed shrews are tiny carnivores, active all year in all mountain zones.

Various types of mice, lemmings, and voles also live on Mount Washington, Katahdin, and on the other Northeast summits. These rodents are herbivores and feed on whatever vegetable food they can find, including sedges, grasses, seeds, and berries of high-elevation plants. Mice have large ears and eyes and long tails. Lemmings and voles have smaller ears and eyes, short tails, and usually longer fur. You can find some member of this family (which also includes rats and muskrats) anywhere in North America. Common lowland species such as meadow voles and white-footed mice get quite high up the mountains; the latter is likely to enter buildings. Brownish-gray northern bog lemmings are active day and night and live in subalpine and alpine meadows in northern New England, New York, Canada, and Alaska. They are rare in our mountains, so if you see a four-inch, rounded, mouse-like creature with concealed ears and a short tail in the sedge meadows, you have made a rare discovery. Yellow-nose voles also inhabit alpine meadows. They have a similar shape, size, and color but with bright yellow noses and longer tails.

▲ Southern red-backed vole is one of at least five species of voles that live on Northeast alpine summits.

THEY'RE HERE!
Animal sightings in the alpine zone may be rare, but signs of their presence are easier to find. Look for scat, burrows, nests, tracks and other clues to creatures above treeline.
snowshoe hare scat
vole nest
vole scat
vole tunnel

porcupine scat
rodent gnaw marks
woodchuck burrow
fox scat
moose scat
marten scat

Insects and Spiders

INSECTS ABOVE TREELINE are intriguing subjects, bringing swarms of entomologists to Mount Washington in the 19th century. One entomologist reported 22 different species of butterflies on the highest summits. One of the earliest and most proficient entomologists to explore the White Mountains was Annie T. Slosson, who recorded 500 different species of flies in the Mount Washington alpine zone in the 1890s.

▲ Many insects feed on pollen and nectar from alpine flowers. This orange-belted bumblebee *(Bombus ternarius)* is pollinating Cutler's goldenrod on New York's Whiteface Mountain.

How do insects survive the weather conditions there? They wait for the sun to give them sufficient body heat. On sunny days in July, a half dozen different kinds of butterfly flit across the summer alpine landscape, searching out flowers, though only three species are endemic—found only in the New England alpine zone—each being worthy of protection. One of these endemic species is the White Mountain butterfly, *Oeneis melissa semidea*, which can be seen mating in the Alpine Garden on calm summer days. Between flights from rock to rock, they can be carefully photographed. Individuals shoot up from their resting places as you approach and sail quickly off with the wind. As striped caterpillars, they feed on Bigelow's sedge. Mount Washington is also home to an endemic variety of the orange-and-black fritillary *(Boloria chariclea montinus)*.

Relatives in the same genus live in alpine and arctic regions in much of the world, including the Rocky Mountains and the Alps.

The other Northeast mountain summits have their share of insects, too. Tiger swallowtails and monarch butterflies can be seen on high ridges. Katahdin is home to the third endemic butterfly species of the New England alpine zone: *Oeneis polyxenes katahdin,* the Katahdin arctic butterfly. This small, mottled butterfly is well-camouflaged among the alpine rocks and lichens.

▲ Predators and plant eaters abound above treeline—a daddy long legs (top) hunts other insects and Gonioctena beetles feed on willows (above).

A number of alpine plants are pollinated by butterflies. Moss campion's pink flowers have narrow nectar-holding tubes and can only be pollinated by these long-tongued insects. Other plants, like Labrador tea, are pollinated by solitary bumblebees. Most flowers in the alpine zone are pollinated by flies, of which there is a large variety. Tiny, biting, early season blackflies are the scourge of humans in the mountains. Later there are nonbiting bee flies, which mimic stinging striped bees but have two wings, not four.

In late August on Mount Washington, White Mountain butterflies are no longer in evidence. Look for green-and-black-striped wingless mountain grasshoppers, *Booneacris glacialis,* which mate on the rocks. Wolf spiders, common throughout summer, are busy hunting prey. Their dark color helps them absorb precious solar heat. Butterfly and moth caterpillars feed on alpine plants. Great and Saint Lawrence tiger moths have large, multicolored "woolly bear" caterpillars. Both are arctic species that overwinter on the New England alpine summits as caterpillars. This is the southern limit to their range.

Little has been written for the public on alpine insects, much less those of the Northeast summits, but Ann Zwinger and Beatrice Willard discuss insect pollinators in their book *Land Above the Trees* (Boulder, CO: Johnson Books, 1996). The Mount Washington Museum, on the summit, has an insect exhibit. It tells about the muscid fly, *Phaonia rugia,* which is found only at and above treeline and feeds on the pollen of mountain avens. The adult life of the fly coincides with the flowering of this plant. The larva of a wingless scorpion fly, *Boreus brumalis,* is reported to feed on mosses.

A muscid fly, found only above treeline, feeds on pollen of mountain avens.▼

More information is needed about these important alpine dwellers. Watch the alpine pollinators and other insect and spider life on a warm, sunny day and see what you can discover.

Alpine Pollinators

If you are lucky enough to be on an alpine summit on a sunny summer day with low wind, the activity around the blooming plants can amaze you. Squadrons of insects—from large butterflies to tiny beetles—are busily looking for food and pollinating flowers.

Native bees, including bumblebees, are common pollinators. They look for ultraviolet strips, invisible to the human eye, on some flowers as guides to nectar and pollen. You'll see many kinds of flies around alpine flowers. They are able to work in cooler temperatures and lower light conditions than bees and are important pollinators in the alpine zone.

Some plants, such as the beautiful blue harebell, receive fewer visits from pollinators above treeline than at lower elevations. Researchers have found, however, that the alpine harebells have sticky stigmas that are receptive to pollen for a longer period. This compensates for lower visitation, allowing pollination to still succeed.

▲ Bumblebees (top) and flies are common pollinators in the alpine zone. Black-and-yellow stripes on syrphid flies (above) mimic bee coloring.

Spiders in the Alpine Zone

If you are fortunate enough to be on top of Mount Washington or Katahdin on a sunny summer day without high winds, you may see alpine wolf spiders on the prowl. Nineteenth-century entomologist Annie T. Slosson found a great many arachnid species on Mount Washington. Only a small number of these are truly alpine, and for some the New England mountains are the southern edge of their ranges.

The wolf spiders belong to a special family, the Lycosids; the name is from an ancient Greek word for

▲ Web-builders above treeline, like this rock orb weaver spider, must act quickly, and rebuild often, during periods of low wind and dry, warm weather to catch their prey.

"wolf." There are at least three species on our highest mountains, and here they are often black. On warm days, they can be seen on bright-colored lichen rocks. They are successful predators and hunt alone. Some chase their victims and pounce, and some wait at the top of their burrows for passing prey. Their eight eyes in three rows give them excellent vision. Unlike web spiders, female wolf spiders carry their egg sacs attached to their spinnerets, the organs that produce silk. After baby spiderlings emerge from their case, they climb up the legs of their mother and cling to her abdomen.

Another alpine arachnid is the rock orb weaver spider, *Aculepeira carbonarioides,* found on Katahdin and Mount Washington as well as the Rocky Mountains. It spins webs among felsenmeer rocks while winds are low and insects are active.

White Mountain fritillary, *Boloria chariclea montinus* · One of three endangered butterflies endemic to northeastern mountains; found only in the alpine zone of the Presidential Range; typical fritillary orange-black-white coloration; studied by biologists Brendan Collins and Spencer Hardy on Mount Washington; helps pollinate mid-summer flowers

Katahdin arctic butterfly, *Oeneis polixenes katahdin* · Endemic to the summit of Katahdin, protected under the Endangered Species Act; close relatives found in arctic tundra from Alaska to Labrador; flies on calm July days; caterpillar is dark-colored with lengthwise light stripes, feeds on sedges and grasses

Eastern swallowtail butterfly, *Papilio glaucus* · Found on all Northeast alpine peaks as well as in gardens and lowland habitats; wingspan of 3"–5" or longer, a surprising sight in the alpine zone; male is always yellow, but the female has both yellow and black forms; can be seen pollinating alpine flowers

White Mountain butterfly, *Oeneis melissa semidea* · The White Mountain butterfly is a true alpine dweller. It is found only at the highest elevations—in the Presidential Range of the White Mountains, from Mount Adams to the Bigelow Lawn. Unlike the monarch butterfly, which occasionally appears on the alpine summits, the White Mountain butterfly does not migrate.

In 1875, Walter Hoxie of the Cambridge Entomological Club reported that this "eagerly sought" butterfly was found near the Mount Washington summit. "They have the peculiar habit of flattening their wings down upon the ground or rock when they alight to avoid the wind," he wrote. He observed that the caterpillars live in a "coarse kind of sedge" and that the adults fly from late June to late July, mainly when the weather is sunny with temperatures over 45°F and wind under 40 mph.

Annie T. Slosson, the late-19th-century entomologist, made annual trips to Mount Washington "in rough costume, with net in hand," and wryly dubbed herself a "rare alpine aberration." She delighted in the ability of the White Mountain butterflies to live in an environment that humans found too severe. Butterfly expert Kent McFarland has reported an adult feeding on mountain sandwort. Moss campion is another of its nectar flowers.

White Mountain butterflies lay their eggs on Bigelow's sedge, and the caterpillars (shown above) feed and grow on this species. They pupate in winter under moss, rocks, or soil in the heart of the alpine zone. It takes two winters before they emerge from their chrysalises as adult butterflies.

Saint Lawrence tiger moth, *Platarctia parthenos* · Caterpillar eats alder, birches, and willows; overwinters in the alpine zone; adult moth flies from June to August; tiger moths are in family Arctiidae with 11,000 species worldwide; these moths are highly colored; this one has orange-and-black-striped hindwings

Great tiger moth, *Arctia caja* · Caterpillar feeds on willows in the alpine zone; turns into a nocturnal moth with brown-and-white patterned forewings and orange hindwings with black spots; can be over 1" long; widespread in Canada and the Pacific Northwest, the Rockies and Labrador, south to New York

Arctic moth, *Anarta nigrolunata* · Small day-flying noctuid moth with mottled gray forewings; hindwings black with a large white spot and white fringe; in the Rocky Mountains and Northern Cascades, found near melting snowdrifts; also found from Alaska to Labrador south to New Mexico; a relict population on Mount Washington

Rock orb weaver spider, *Aculepeira carbonarioides* · Found in mountain boulder field crevices throughout much of Canada and Alaska, as well as Colorado, Maine, and New Hampshire; look for it in subalpine talus slopes on Katahdin and alpine felsenmeer on Mount Washington where webs are especially vulnerable to damaging wind and rain.

Wolf spiders. · There are 2,000 wolf spider species, family Lycosidae, the most diverse group of spiders in alpine and arctic sites; several are often seen on Mount Washington on warm days; eight eyes in three rows provide excellent eyesight; all wolf spiders are predators—some at night, some in the day; female spiders carry egg sacs attached by spinnerets, newly hatched spiders ride on their mothers' backs

Crab spider · Family Thomisidae; so-called for their two front pairs of legs and ability to scuttle sideways; these predators ambush insects on or beside flowers; powerful front legs grab prey and hold it to paralyze with a venomous bite

Wingless mountain grasshopper, *Booneacris glacialis* · Small wingless grasshopper found in Minnesota and Ontario, east to New Brunswick, Maine, and New Hampshire, and south through the Appalachians; can be abundant in White Mountain and Katahdin alpine zones in late summer, especially in snowbed communities; adults feed on leafy vegetation; first described from top of Mount Madison by Harvard entomologist Samuel Scudder in 1862; male (right) and female (below) have different coloring; males (5⁄8") are smaller than females (3⁄4"); sometimes called "White Mountain locust;" belongs to the spur-throated grasshopper subfamily, *Meanoplinae*

Ground beetle, *Carabus chamissonis* · A rare beetle found on Mount Washington; one entomologist named this population *Carabus chamissonis washingtoni*; the more common alpine ground beetle, *Amara hyperborea*, is on the southern tip of its range on Mount Washington

Dragonfly nymph · suborder Anisoptera; the presence of dragonfly nymphs (larvae) at or above treeline indicates that adults lay eggs in high elevation lakes and bogs; nymphs prey on underwater insects and amphibian tadpoles.

Caddisfly larva · There are 12,000 caddisflies in the order Trichoptera; adults are moth-like, with two pairs of membranous wings; aquatic larvae build protective cases using silk and sand, twigs, stones, or in this case, mica; occurs in many aquatic habitats and zones, including streams in the Alpine Garden and Lakes of the Clouds on Mount Washington, as shown here

CONSERVATION of our rare and interesting alpine flora and fauna should be the concern of all who enjoy the Northeast's mountains. There are many ways we can help—or prevent future harm to—the very special alpine ecosystems. Conservation of the rare plants of the White Mountains has been a major concern of AMC and other private and government agencies since at least the 1930s. At that time, botanists Stuart K. Harris and Fred Steele warned against the mass collecting of rare plants that had occurred over the past century. Plants were not the only victims. Annie T. Slosson wrote in 1893 about the beetle collectors: "The summit looked as if shaken by an earthquake, the ground was full of holes and pits of irregular shapes, from which heavy stones had been dragged by the . . . eager collectors. . . . Alpine beetles were in serious danger of extinction."

While you're on the mountain, the rules for protecting alpine species are simple: Do not pick any flowers or disturb creatures on these mountaintops. Stay on the trails and within designated areas near the huts. Do not take rock samples; doing so can disturb the special habitats of both plants and animals.

Before popular photography, tourists and botanists collected specimens of alpine plants for souvenirs and study. This the first published photograph of Cutler's goldenrod from Pease's 1924 book, *Vascular Flora of Coos County.* ▼

Success Story—Robbins' Cinquefoil

The Robbins' or dwarf cinquefoil (p. 70) is one of the Northeast's rarest plants, an endemic species that occurs only in the alpine zone of the White Mountains and nowhere else in the world. In 1980, it was officially listed as a federally endangered species. It was then known to grow mainly in Monroe Flats—the saddle between Mount Monroe and Mount Washington; a small population on Franconia Ridge was rediscovered in 1984. An earlier known population near Mount Lafayette was extirpated by 1915. Robbins' cinquefoil is one of the first alpine plants to bloom in spring; its yellow flowers appear in late May to early June, just after the snow melts. This diminutive plant lives at an elevation of over 5,000 feet on Monroe Flats in the harshest of winter conditions, with temperatures of −40°F and exposure to extremely high winds, abrasive ice, and blowing snow. It grows in barren soil subject to frost heaving but is aided by its long taproot. Few other plants can survive these conditions; Robbins' cinquefoil is a good competitor in its own special niche. Even so, it needs eight to thirteen years to reach flowering size.

▲ The original route of the Crawford Path up Mount Washington crossed through the main population of rare Robbins' cinquefoil, exposing it to trampling by people and horses. Illustration from *Harper's Weekly*, 1869

Robbins' cinquefoil was first collected at Monroe Flats in 1824 by Thomas Nuttall, an early plant and bird explorer. William Oakes and Charles Pickering found it the following year, and many other botanists collected it zealously in the 1800s; some sent or even sold specimens to herbaria all over the world.

In the 20th century, trampling pushed Robbins' cinquefoil closer to the edge of extinction. Monroe

▲ Recovery efforts for Robbins' cinquefoil included growing new plants from collected seed and transplanting them to their alpine sites.

Flats is on the original route of the Crawford Path, constructed by Abel Crawford in 1918 for both people and horse traffic. In 1983, both the Crawford Path and the Dry River Trail were rerouted away from Robbins' cinquefoil's critical habitat. A low scree wall was built to protect the habitat, and no one is admitted to this site without a permit.

Activities to try to recover its population began as early as 1979. A plan, devised in 1983 and revised in 1991, had several strategies beyond protecting the remaining plants from further threats. Four transplant sites were set up; earlier such attempts had largely failed. Studies of the Robbins' cinquefoil's basic biology enabled researchers to collect seeds on the alpine sites, to grow plants from this seed, and in early July to set out the young plants in new, suitable sites. Two transplant sites succeeded, on Franconia Ridge and Monroe Flats. Seeds were also collected for a permanent seed bank at the New England Wild Flower Society (now Native Plant Trust) in Framingham, Massachusetts, where they continue to research this rare plant's propagation.

The plan succeeded. On Monroe Flats the number of well-established Robbins' cinquefoil plants went from 1,547 in 1983 to 4,575 in 1999. In 2002, the U.S. Fish and Wildlife Service determined that Robbins' cinquefoil was no longer an endangered species and removed it from the official "List of Endangered and Threatened Plants" under the Endangered Species Act. The White Mountain National Forest and AMC continue to maintain the scree-walled area protecting the Monroe Flats habitat. A follow-up count by AMC indicates that the Monroe Flats and transplant populations continue to expand without the protections that had been provided when they were considered endangered and threatened.

Robbins' cinquefoil habitat is closed off to protect plants from trampling. ▼

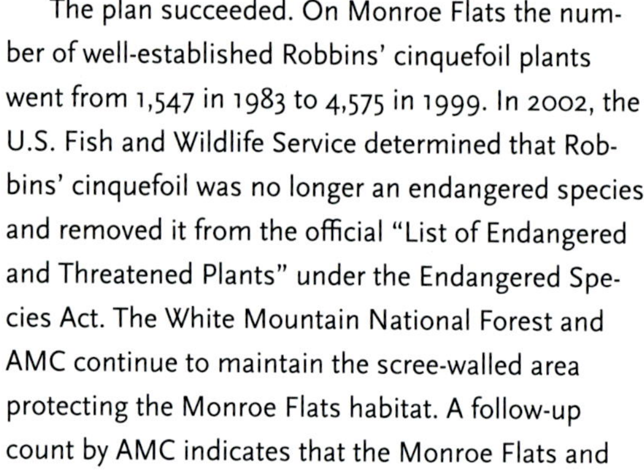

This is an amazing success story, a different kind of "mountain rescue." It is only the second plant ever to be taken off the endangered species list because of its recovery.

Summit Stewardship

The hiking boom in the 1960s and 1970s brought a surge of climbers to the Northeast's high mountains. On alpine summits, piles of trash, tent sites, camp fires, and the crush of thousands of new Vibram soles on uncontrolled herd paths killed plants, removed soil, and exposed large areas of bedrock.

In the Adirondacks, in the late 1960s, Dr. Edwin H. Ketchledge, along with hundreds of other volunteers, pioneered a restoration program for impacted alpine vegetation. Rocks were placed along damaged trailsides and lowland grasses planted in eroded areas so their roots would stabilize the soil. Gradually mosses invaded and provided a seedbed for mountain sandwort and other native alpine plants. The introduced grasses could not survive the nutrient-poor alpine soils and died out. This successful program was continued for over twenty years.

▲ In trampled areas on New York's Alquonguin Peak, rocks were placed along eroded edges to stabilize soil.

Ketchledge's efforts to protect the alpine zone did not end there, however. In 1989, he organized a group of individuals from the Adirondack Nature Conservancy, Adirondack Mountain Club, New York State Department of Environmental Conservation, the Adirondack Forty-Sixers, and other interested parties to discuss creating an educational presence on the summits. Out of this meeting, the Adirondack High Peaks Summit Stewardship Program was born.

Today there are summit steward programs in place on the highest alpine peaks in New York, Vermont, New Hampshire and Maine. During the warmer months and into the fall season, trained educators greet hikers and urge them to stay on the trails and off the fragile terrain. One summit steward recalls hearing a child on top of Mount Mansfield call to her father, "Don't step there! It's not grass; it's rare plants!" Summit stewards share trail and weather information, do trail work, and contribute to scientific projects on their mountains.

▲ A summit steward on Whiteface points out alpine plants to visitors.

Blazes and string direct hikers on Mount Mansfield. ▼

Education is important for conservation. The authors of this field guide published it, and earlier ones for both the New England and Adirondack alpine summits, for just this purpose. Mountain clubs and conservation organizations offer a wealth of programs by naturalists about alpine ecology, and there are many resources online. Hikers who get to know the amazing alpine plants and animals will care about their protection.

In addition to stewardship and education, physical infrastructure helps enforce conservation efforts. Trail signs, scree walls, rock paving, and bog bridging are all used to direct foot traffic and protect rare plants above treeline. On Mount Mansfield, where rocks are unavailable, white string cordons are used to guide hikers along trail routes.

In 2025 the Randolph Mountain Club was awarded a grant from the Waterman Foundation for work on Lowe's Path, built in 1875 in the northern Presidential Range alpine zone. The experienced RMC trail crew repaired the treadway to keep hikers on the trail and off fragile alpine vegetation. They blocked herd paths, built cairns, rock steps, and scree walls, and cut back krummholz to make the original trail clear. Additional work on Lowe's Path will be done in future seasons.

▲ Herd paths and shortcuts erode summit soil down to bedrock, killing alpine plants.

Climate Change

A great deal of attention has been devoted recently to climate change and its effects on the Northeast's alpine flora and fauna. One study showed that treelines in the Presidential Range and on Mount Katahdin have risen in elevation an average of three meters per decade for the past 40 years. The AMC's Northeast Alpine Flower Watch program monitors the dates on which several key alpine plants flower, tracking climate-driven changes and finding that plants appear to be flowering one to two days earlier than they did historically. As on alpine summits elsewhere in the world, climate change seems to be driving increases in shrubs and declines in mosses and some herbaceous plants. Long-term monitoring now is being done on a regular basis in the White Mountains and in two mountain ranges in Québec—the Chic-Chocs and the Uapishka—recording changes and trying to understand the relationships among warming and

▲ Bloom times for snowbed species like moss plant are linked to snowmelt dates and may be affected by warming temperatures.

other conditions. An additional monitoring site is also being planned in the Adirondacks.

Of the many and varied alpine communities presented in this book, snowbed communities have proved most vulnerable to climate change. In several alpine areas in Europe, where the temperature rise has been greater than on the Northeast's mountains, the snow melts sooner, adversely affecting some of the specially adapted snowbed flowering plants and alpine mosses.

With so much potential for change on our doorstep, it seemed worthwhile to do baseline studies of New England's alpine snowbed communities that could be revisited with ongoing climate change. In 2012, Nancy Slack was awarded a Waterman Fund grant to do such a study in alpine areas on Mount Washington. A team of researchers worked on the snowbed and the related streamside communities in the Alpine Garden and on the summit cone. In addition to identifying and quantifying all the plants currently in the snowbed communities, the study participants also used GPS to log locations of populations of rare mosses and lichens in snowbed and other Mount Washington plant communities for future monitoring.

All the flowering plants, ferns, mosses, and lichens of the area's snowbed communities are included in the study, which also records the length of snow lie and other factors. Rare flowering plants and mosses have already been identified. Some, though not all, of these species are specialized for snowbed environments. A number of plants that live in the lower mountain zones, such as bluebead lily, bunchberry, and Canada mayflower, are able to grow in the alpine snowbed communities as well, but that will be true only as long as the snow cover in these areas persists late into the spring season. If higher temperatures cause it to melt earlier, these communities will change. The specialist plants that are able to live only in snowbeds will suffer as well.

Research

The Northeast mountains are the focus of many ongoing scientific projects—high-elevation birds, bees, mosses, lichens, insects, and more, are all currently being studied. Photo point monitoring projects, showing change over time, are underway in the Adirondacks, Mount Mansfield, and the Presidential Range.

In New Hampshire, the endemic White Mountain Arctic butterfly and the White Mountain fritillary (see pages 171–172) are the focus of a collaboration led by New

White Mountain fritillaries mating on Mount Washington. This is one of several rare butterflies being studied on alpine peaks in Maine and New Hampshire. ▼

Hampshire Fish and Game biologist Heidi Holman. Their ongoing field surveys and lab work have yielded a better understanding of the butterflies' habitat use, host plants, life history, and population numbers. The results will help support and improve conservation of these rare species, and identify threats, including habitat loss and climate change.

On Mount Mansfield, Desiree Narango leads a team of scientists from the Vermont Center for Ecostudies that has been tracking populations of Bicknell's thrush and other high-elevation breeding birds for 30 years. Using mist nets along the summit ridgeline, each summer nearly 1,000 birds are banded, catalogued, and some fitted with nanotags, to assess changes in the breeding bird populations. Research shows that two species familiar to hikers above treeline—slate-colored juncos and white-throated sparrows—are fast declining in the southern part of their range.

Nineteenth-century bridle paths and carriage roads to mountain summits were strewn with horse manure that contained seeds of lowland plants—some sprouted in protected spots. ▼

Invasive Plants

The surge of trail building and summit development on Northeast summits in the late 19th century, began the introduction of non-native invasive plants into the areas above treeline. On Mount Washington, Mount Mansfield, and Whiteface Mountain horses carried tourists and pulled wagons, and left droppings loaded with seeds from their meals at the base. Construction of summit houses and huts disturbed alpine soils making them vulnerable to seedling invasion.

In July 1902, hiker Emma Coleman observed "dandelions

▲ Alpine snowbed infested with dandelions on Mount Washington in 2014.

were in bloom at the Appalachian Mt. Club hut at the foot of Mt. Madison."[2] Throughout the 20th century, non-native species, mainly of Eurasian origin, slowly increased around Mount Washington's summit structures, including the railway line. Their seeds arrived in the treads of upward bound tires on dirt, and later, paved roads. The buildings enabled lowland plants by reflecting heat and deflecting killing wind. In the 1990s, hawkweed, yarrow, and dandelions had formed a four-mile ribbon up the Mount Washington auto road verge.

For a time, it was generally thought that lowland species would not persist beyond the bounds of the protective summit infrastructure. In 2014, however, an alarming discovery of thousands of dandelions, *Taraxacum officinale*, robust and well-established in a series of alpine snowbeds on Mount

Volunteers hand dig dandelions invading an alpine sedge meadow on Mount Washington. ▼

A few of the invasive non-native plants considered high priority for monitoring and removal in the Northeast's alpine areas. ▼

Washington, prompted a survey and control effort led by the White Mountain Forest Service. This work led to the first detailed study of non-native species in the New Hampshire alpine zone and contributed to the first invasive management plan for an alpine zone in eastern North America.[3] Going forward, the AMC will monitor and control invasive plants around their high huts.

On Whiteface Mountain, the road to the summit has provided a vector for non-native flora, all the way into the parking lot below the summit. Near the summit tower is the site of one of New York's rarest plants, a population of Boott's rattlesnakeroot (pg. 79). The area is significantly infested with many non-native species, all competing for space, pollinators and other resources on the mountaintop.

To date, the Katahdin alpine zone remains free of non-native plants, protected by its remoteness and lack of development. Mount Marcy is similarly buffered, but recently dandelions have been reported from its alpine area. Around the world, dandelions and other invasive plants threaten alpine areas in Alaska, Australia, Asia, and the Andes.

MOUNTAIN PLANT PHENOLOGY

PHENOLOGY IS THE STUDY of recurring natural phenomena. It can apply to animals—the migration of birds, the spawning of fish, or the emergence of insects—but phenology most often refers to the responses of plants to seasonal changes in their environments. Throughout the year, day length, solar intensity, temperature, ice and snow cover, wind velocities, and many other environmental factors change. Nowhere in the Northeast are these changes more spectacular than above treeline. In the alpine zone these changes are extreme: from harsh winter winds, ice, and very low temperatures to summer days of brilliant sun, which bring out the butterflies even on Mount Washington's summit. The ground itself is in flux as repeated freezing and thawing causes dramatic soil movements that make it difficult for new plants to become established. Many of these factors are cyclical; the number of hours of daylight (versus darkness) is the same on any particular date every year; other factors such as snowfall vary annually.

Diapensia's foliage turns red in fall and remains so until flowering in early June.▼

Both plants and animals use environmental cues in relation to seasonal changes important for their

▲ Because it grows at a range of elevations, bunchberry can be in flower high on the mountain and in fruit lower down.

behavior and reproduction. The number of hours of day and night, usually termed day length, cues hormonal changes that influence reproduction and migration in birds. Day length also is important in initiating flowering, autumn colors, and leaf fall in plants. It is fascinating and important to study cyclical events in the lives of organisms and determine how they relate to seasonal weather patterns and other aspects of the environment.

Like any observant mountain hiker, you have probably made phenological observations yourself, simply by noticing how plants look different in spring and fall. Plant names themselves may be expressions of seasonal change.

One attractive plant found at all mountain elevations in the Northeast has two common names, dwarf cornel and bunchberry. In spring and early summer this plant displays four white bracts surrounding a cluster of tiny flowers; it looks like a small version of the flowering dogwood tree. Both originally had the same Latin name, *Cornus*—thus dwarf cornel—though the alpine plant is now officially known as *Chamaepericlymenum canadensis*. In the late summer and fall this plant sheds its white bracts, and the central flowers develop into brilliant red berries, hence the name "bunchberry." Because many environmental factors change with elevation, the stages, or phenology, of this plant occur at different times during the growing season. So when it is just beginning to flower at higher elevations, it will already be in fruit at lower elevations.

The phenology and natural history of Robbins' cinquefoil has been carefully studied. It is one of the first plants to flower just after snowmelt in the alpine zone, sometimes by mid-May. In full bloom an individual plant, no more than one inch high, can have up to 40 yellow flowers. June is its main flowering time; by mid-July it is in fruit, with its one-seeded fruits, or achenes, ripe by mid-July. Windy days in late July help the fruits of the Robbins' cinquefoil separate from the flower head. Seeds usually fall nearby but do not germinate until the following June or July. Because of the harsh conditions of their alpine habitat, the young plant takes many years to grow large enough to flower and fruit, but smaller plants also show phenological changes—their new leaves expand in spring and seedlings shed their cotyledon leaves by the end of their first growing season.

By July, Robbins' cinquefoil has set seed; in August its leaves begin to turn color.▼

Mountain cranberry blooms in June and produces ripe fruit in August. ▼

The alpine plant illustrated here and on page 92 is usually called mountain cranberry in New York and New England, but lingonberry in Europe. It is a ground-hugging shrub with round, shiny evergreen leaves with light-pink bell-shaped flowers. It lives in the alpine zone but in more sheltered conditions than diapensia or Robbins' cinquefoil. Its evergreen leaves give it a different phenology from alpine plants that shed their leaves in winter. Mountain cranberry can start to photosynthesize early in the growing season since it doesn't need to put out an entire set of new leaves. Later in the season its dazzling red berries are hard to miss.

Northeast Alpine Flower Watch Program

With this field guide for reference, hone your naturalist skills and collect valuable information for an ongoing study of our alpine areas. The Northeast Alpine Flower Watch program is a partnership between the Appalachian Mountain Club, Adirondack Mountain Club, Green Mountain Club, and Baxter State Park.

Use the iNaturalist app to share photos of targeted plants from the Northeast's alpine areas—including bog bilberry, Bigelow's sedge, mountain avens, diapensia, mountain cranberry, and Labrador tea. Your photo data will indicate flowering and fruiting times, and will contribute to a regional data set to help determine impacts of a warming climate.

Plants in alpine environments act as sensitive bioindicators of climate change. Scientists are paying careful attention to alpine and arctic ecosystems, and other groups are monitoring these same targeted species in locations all over the world.

Labrador tea, one of the targeted species in the Northeast Alpine Flower Watch program, blooming above treeline in mid-July. ▼

Flowering Times in the Alpine Zone

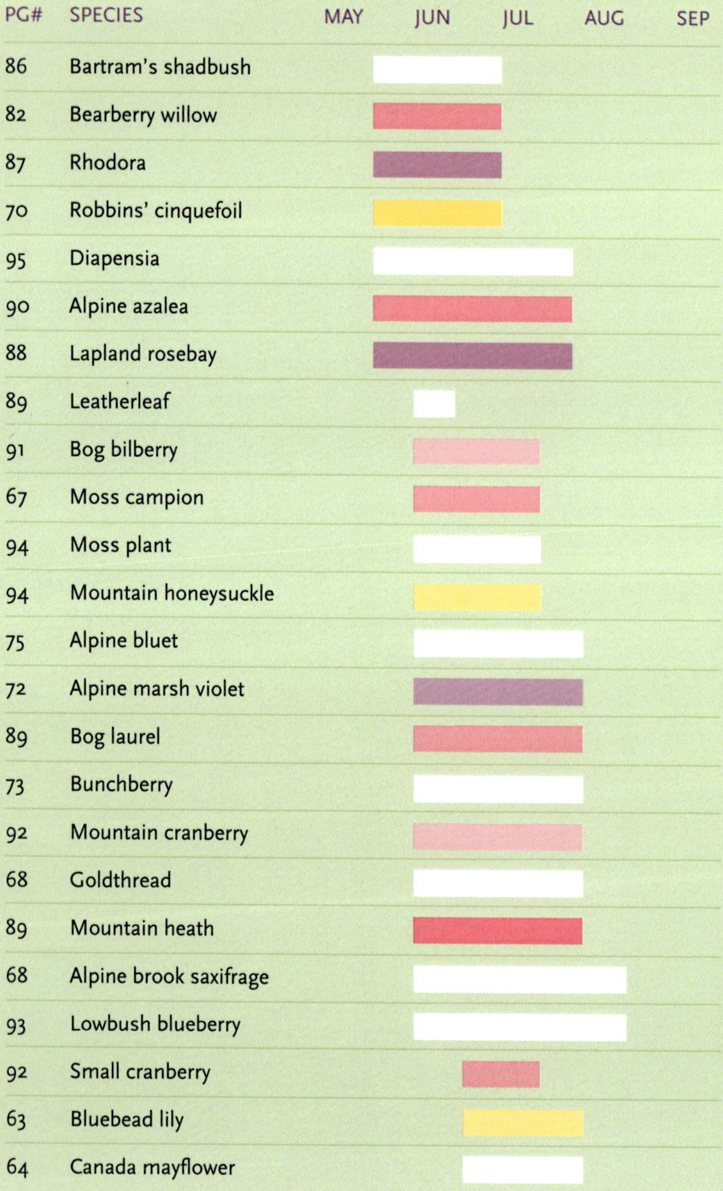

PG#	SPECIES	MAY	JUN	JUL	AUG	SEP
86	Bartram's shadbush					
82	Bearberry willow					
87	Rhodora					
70	Robbins' cinquefoil					
95	Diapensia					
90	Alpine azalea					
88	Lapland rosebay					
89	Leatherleaf					
91	Bog bilberry					
67	Moss campion					
94	Moss plant					
94	Mountain honeysuckle					
75	Alpine bluet					
72	Alpine marsh violet					
89	Bog laurel					
73	Bunchberry					
92	Mountain cranberry					
68	Goldthread					
89	Mountain heath					
68	Alpine brook saxifrage					
93	Lowbush blueberry					
92	Small cranberry					
63	Bluebead lily					
64	Canada mayflower					

PG#	SPECIES	MAY	JUN	JUL	AUG	SEP
88	Labrador tea					
64	Rose twisted stalk					
91	Dwarf bilberry					
70	Mountain avens					
66	Mountain sandwort					
69	Three-toothed cinquefoil					
66	Alpine bistort					
64	Clasping-leaved twisted stalk					
74	Alpine speedwell					
66	Mountain sorrel					
74	Pale painted cup					
73	Alpine willow-herb					
79	Boott's rattlesnake-root					
63	False hellebore					
74	Starflower					
65	Tall leafy white orchid					
85	Northern meadowsweet					
79	Arnica					
76	Harebell					
77	Purple-stemmed aster					
67	Boreal stitchwort					
79	Three-leaved rattlesnake-root					
76	Large-leaved goldenrod					
77	Cutler's goldenrod					
77	Sharp-leaved wood aster					

◀ Mountain heath with bunchberry and Canada may-flower in an alpine snowbed on Mount Washington

SELECTED REFERENCES

Allen, Bruce. *Maine Mosses,* Volumes 1 and 2. New York Botanical Garden, 2014.

Bell, Allison, and Maida Goodwin. *Glorious Mouintain Days.* Bondcliff Books, 2018.

Bliss, Lawrence C. *Alpine Zone of the Presidential Range.* Boston: Appalachian Mountain Club, 1963.

Brodo, Irwin, and Sylvia and Stephen Sharnoff. *Lichens of North America.* Yale University Press, 2001.

Haines, Arthur. *Native Plant Trust's Flora Novae Angliae.* Second edition, 2026. Online.

Hinds, James W., and Patricia L. Hinds. *The Macrolichens of New England.* New York Botanical Garden, 2007.

Huber, J. Parker. *The Wildest Country: Exploring Thoreau's Maine.* Appalachian Mountain Club, 2008.

Jones, Mike, and Liz Willey. *Eastern Alpine Guide.* University Press of New England, 2018.

McKnight, Karl B., Joseph R. Rohrer, Kristen McKnight Ward, and Warren J. Perdrizet. *Common Mosses of the Northeast and Appalachians.* Princeton University Press, 2013.

Mittelhauser, Glen H., Jensen Bissell, Don Cameron, Alison C. Dibble, Arthur Haines, Jean Hoekwater, Marilee Lovit and Aaron Megquier. *The Plants of Baxter State Park.* University of Maine Press, 2016.

Pope, Ralph. *Lichens above Treeeline: A Hiker's Guide to Treeline Zone Lichens of the Northeastern States.* University Press of New England, 2005.

Waterman, Laura, and Guy Waterman. *Forest and Crag: A History of Hiking, Trail Blazing, and Adventure in the Northeast Mountains,* 2nd edition. Appalachian Mountain Club, 2003.

Zwinger, Ann H., and Beatrice Willard. *Land Above the Trees: A Guide to American Alpine Tundra,* revised edition. Johnson Books, 1996.

Index to species in this field guide

Bold page references indicate primary descriptions and/or photos for species.

◄ Mountain avens, *Geum peckii*, on the headwall of the Great Gulf below Mount Jefferson.

IMAGE CREDITS by page number: 22, ©The Schlesinger Library, Radcliffe Institute, Harvard University; 51, ©Sally Naser; 69, middle, ©Arthur Haines; 109, top, ©Emily Schmieder; 113, top, ©Des Callaghan; 146, top–bottom ©Wayne Oakes, Tim Olson, Cody Limber—Cornell Lab of Ornithology | Macaulay Library; 147, both ©Kent McFarland; 148, all ©Jeff Nadler; 149, top–bottom ©Jeff Nadler, ©Jeff Nadler, ©Peter Paul—Cornell Lab of Ornithology | Macaulay Library; 150, all ©Jeff Nadler; 151, all ©Jeff Nadler; 152, all ©Jeff Nadler; 153, top and bottom ©Jeff Nadler, middle ©Kent McFarland; 153, top ©Olivier Gilg, bottom ©Larry Master; 160, both ©Sally Naser; 171, middle ©Rob Tice; 172, middle Heidi Holman; 185, ©Kent McFarland; back cover, third down, ©Jeff Nadler

END NOTES

1. Joshua Henry Huntington et al., *Mount Washington in winter, or the experiences of a scientific expedition upon the highest mountain in New England, 1870–71*, Chick and Andrews, 1871.

2. Marian M. Pychowska, "Two in the Alpine Pastures," *Appalachia*, December, 1888.

3. Bell, Allison, and Maida Goodwin, *Glorious Mountain Days*, Bondcliff Books, 2018.

4. Nichols, W., D. Sperduto, R. Esch, and L. Costello. 2025. *Alpine Invasive Plant Species Early Detection and Rapid Response Plan.* Report prepared by NH Natural Heritage Bureau, Division of Forests & Lands, DNCR, Concord, NH.

THANKS to Bob Capers for support and scientific contributions; to Leslie Harris, Sally Naser, Laura Shores, and Nicky Pizzo for help on mountain research; to Des Callaghan, Olivier Gilg, Arthur Haines, Cody Limber, Larry Master, Kent McFarland, Jeff Nadler, Sally Naser, Wayne Oakes, Tim Olson, Peter Paul, Emily Schmieder, and Rob Tice for contributions to photography; to Doug Weihrauch for data in the flowering chart; to Heidi Holman, Georgia Murray, Desirée Narango, Heather Siart, Nava Tabak, and Jordan Toureville for information about current research; to David Bosse, Mike Jones, and Ben Kimball for editing assistance.

Bell and Slack in the Alpine Garden

AUTHORS

Allison W. Bell is a designer and photographer in western Massachusetts. She is author, with Maida Goodwin, of *Glorious Mountain Days—the 1902 Hike that Helped Save the White Mountains* (2018). Combined, she and Nancy have enjoyed over 100 years of alpine plants in bloom. Dr. Nancy G. Slack was a plant ecologist and Professor emerita of the Sage Colleges. She is author, with Allison W. Bell, of the prize-winning *Adirondack Alpine Summits, an Ecological Field Guide* (2007) and *Field Guide to the New England Alpine Summits* (2016), and the co-author/ editor of *Bryophyte Ecology and Climate Change* (2011). In 2014 she received the Guy Waterman Alpine Steward Award for lifetime achievement in alpine ecology and conservation work for northeast mountain wilderness.